# Quick
## Scripture
## Reference
### for
# Counseling

## Quick Scripture Reference Books

*Quick Scripture Reference for Counseling* by John G. Kruis

*Quick Scripture Reference for Counseling Women* by Patricia A. Miller

*Quick Scripture Reference for Counseling Youth* by Keith R. Miller and Patricia A. Miller

*Quick Scripture Reference for Counseling Men* by Keith R. Miller

# *Quick*
# SCRIPTURE
# REFERENCE
# for
# Counseling

## EXPANDED EDITION

## JOHN G. KRUIS

**BakerBooks**

*a division of Baker Publishing Group*
Grand Rapids, Michigan

© 1988, 1994, 2000, 2013 by John G. Kruis

Published by Baker Books
a division of Baker Publishing Group
P.O. Box 6287, Grand Rapids, MI 49516-6287
www.bakerbooks.com

Printed in the United States of America

Library of Congress Cataloging-in-Publication Data
Kruis, John G.
     Quick scripture reference for counseling / John G. Kruis. — fourth
edition
          pages cm
     ISBN 978-0-8010-1579-3 (pbk.)
          1. Counseling—Religious aspects—Christianity. 2. Bible—Use. I. Title.
BR115.C69K78 2013
253.5—dc23                                                    2013016571

The author's royalties from the sale of this book are donated to the National Association of Nouthetic Counselors.

14   15   16   17   18   19          7   6   5   4   3

**Compiled for . . .**

your personal benefit, and to help you use the Scriptures more effectively in counseling.

**Dedicated to . . .**

the memory of my wife, Gene, who was a wonderful, faithful pastor's wife and mother. And she, with deep devotion, freely served for several years as the secretary and treasurer of the Biblical Counseling Center in Jenison, Michigan, which we founded together in 1982.

All Scripture is God-breathed and is useful for
teaching, rebuking, correcting and training in
righteousness, so that the man of God may
be thoroughly equipped for every good work.

2 Timothy 3:16–17

---

Rev. John G. Kruis passed into his eternal home in November 2010.
We would like to pay tribute to both of our parents, John and
Gene Kruis, who were loving and faithful servants of God and of
his people. For them, the reading and study of the Bible was an
important and delightful part of every day. We are grateful to God
for their example and for their love and devotion to him and to us.

At the beginning of counseling sessions, after listening carefully
to those seeking counsel, Dad would say, "I have good news for
you; there is hope!" Hope came not from what he could do or say
but from the power of God's Word. We pray that this book will
continue to be used as a tool to offer hope to many.

With love and hope in Christ,
Ron, John, Nelva, Kevin, and David

# Subject Guide

## Salvation

### Leading a Person to Christ

I. Apart from Christ we are helpless and sinful.

    A. We are all sinners.

    B. We are in spiritual bondage.

    C. We are alienated from God.

    D. Knowledge of sin comes by the law of God.

    E. God, in his justice, punishes sinners.

    F. We cannot save ourselves in any way.

II. Jesus saves us by grace and through faith.

    A. Jesus suffered and died for sinners.

    B. Examples of those who were saved by grace and through faith.

III. The Lord calls sinners like you and me.

IV. We are saved to joyfully obey and serve the Lord.

# Introduction

## Why This Book?

### For Biblical Counseling

"All Scripture is God-breathed and is useful for teaching, rebuking, correcting and training in righteousness, so that the man of God may be thoroughly equipped for every good work" (2 Tim. 3:16–17). "The word of God is living and active. Sharper than any double-edged sword, it penetrates even to dividing soul and spirit, joints and marrow; it judges the thoughts and attitudes of the heart" (Heb. 4:12).

As you do the Lord's work, the Holy Spirit is always the primary counselor, and he works powerfully, sovereignly through his own Word. He brings people to a conviction of sin and to a saving knowledge of Jesus Christ through his Word. It is by the Scriptures that he teaches them how to love God and their neighbors as themselves, to live a life of faith and obedience in response to his saving grace. Through the Scriptures the Holy Spirit comforts, rebukes, corrects, and trains them in righteousness. In this way people of all ages and from various walks of life are helped; all kinds of personal, marriage, and family problems are resolved—and God is glorified.

It is, therefore, essential for you to be "thoroughly equipped" with the Scriptures, prepared for "every good work." The better equipped you are, the more effective you will be in helping others.

### For Personal, Marriage, and Family Needs

This *Quick Scripture Reference for Counseling* was first published in March of 1988. As the fourth edition goes to press, over 175,000 copies of the English edition have been sold internationally. It has become evident that it is being used for much more than counseling. Many are using the book to help meet their personal, marriage, and family needs, including resolving conflicts within the home. Some are using it as a guide for personal and family devotions.

## The Uniqueness of This Book

This *Quick Scripture Reference for Counseling* is designed especially to help God's people use the Scriptures more effectively in their counseling ministries. It has several distinctive features. Scripture passages and texts are listed under topics. They are arranged so that you can see at a glance the gist and the significance of each text or passage as it relates to the topic under which it is listed. In many instances Bible verses are quoted in their entirety so that you have them immediately before you. When longer passages are listed, often the key verses are quoted.

To maximize the usefulness of the book, the entries under each topic have been numbered so that, as you prepare an agenda for counseling someone, you can easily list several pertinent Bible passages to have right at your fingertips. For example, as you seek to lead a person to the forgiveness of sins, or assurance, you might write on your agenda something like this:

Forgiveness of sins—page 90

1. Believers are made as white as snow. Isa. 1:18.

6. God will not despise a broken spirit and a contrite heart. Ps. 51:17.

9. God calls sinners to seek him and promises them forgiveness when they repent. Isa. 55:6–7.

11. Jesus forgave the penitent woman. Luke 7:36–50.

26. God has lavished his grace on us, choosing us, forgiving us of all our sins through the shed blood of Christ. Eph. 1:3–10.

This feature will also help you to prepare homework assignments that meet the specific needs of each counselee.

My prayer is that this book will help many to use the Scriptures more effectively in counseling others, for their comfort, joy, peace, and eternal well-being, and above all for God's glory.

# Adultery

*If one* continues to live in the state of adultery, see also Sexual Immorality, Warnings, Obedience. If one repents of adultery, see Forgiveness of Sins, Peace.

### 1. Adultery is out of the heart.

**Matthew 15:19** For out of the heart come evil thoughts, murder, adultery, sexual immorality, theft, false witness, slander.

### 2. No adulterers go to heaven.

**1 Corinthians 6:9–10** Do you not know that the unrighteous will not inherit the kingdom of God? Do not be deceived: neither the sexually immoral, nor idolaters, nor adulterers, nor men who practice homosexuality, nor thieves, nor the greedy, nor drunkards, nor revilers, nor swindlers will inherit the kingdom of God.

### 3. God will judge the adulterer.

**Hebrews 13:4** Let marriage be held in honor among all, and let the marriage bed be undefiled, for God will judge the sexually immoral and adulterous.

### 4. Adultery can be avoided.

**Proverbs 4:23**
**Proverbs 4:13–27** *(Stay far from the path of evil.)*
**Proverbs 6:27–28** *(Don't play with fire.)* Can a man carry fire next to his chest and his clothes not be burned? Or can one walk on hot coals and his feet not be scorched?

### 5. Shun adultery.

**Proverbs 6:20–35**

6. The adulteress's snare leads to misery.

    Proverbs 7:1–27

7. The adulteress's snare is a deep pit.

    Proverbs 22:14 The mouth of an adulteress is a deep pit; he who is cursed of the LORD will fall into it. (NASB)

8. David fed the flame.

    2 Samuel 11:2–3 Now when evening came David arose from his bed and walked around on the roof of the king's house, and from the roof he saw a woman bathing; and the woman was very beautiful in appearance. So David sent and inquired about the woman. (NASB)

9. David was depressed before he confessed his sin of adultery.

    Psalm 32:3–5

10. Nathan called David to repent of his adultery.

    2 Samuel 12:1–14 *(The prophet Nathan spoke to David in a parable after he had sinned with Bathsheba.)*

11. David confessed his adultery, and God graciously forgave him.

    Psalm 32; Psalm 51 *(David pleaded for God's forgiveness and expressed his joy after being forgiven.)*

12. God forgives the sin of adultery and frees the sinner from it.

    1 Corinthians 6:11 And such [adulterers, etc.] were some of you. But you were washed, but you were sanctified, but you were justified in the name of the Lord Jesus and by the Spirit of our God. (NKJV)

13. Looking on a woman lustfully is adultery; spiritual surgery is needed.

    Matthew 5:27–30 You have heard that it was said to those of old, "You shall not commit adultery." But I say to you that

whoever looks at a woman to lust for her has already committed adultery with her in his heart. If your right eye causes you
to sin, pluck it out and cast it from you; for it is more profitable
for you that one of your members perish, than for your whole
body to be cast into hell. And if your right hand causes you to
sin, cut it off and cast it from you; for it is more profitable for
you that one of your members perish, than for your whole body
to be cast into hell. (NKJV)

14. **Beware of seductive women.**

    **Proverbs 23:26–28** My son, give me your heart, and let your
    eyes observe my ways. For a prostitute is a deep pit; an adulteress
    is a narrow well. She lies in wait like a robber and increases the
    traitors among mankind.

15. **Stolen water is sweet, but . . .**

    **Proverbs 9:17–18** Stolen water is sweet, and bread eaten in
    secret is pleasant. But he does not know that the dead are there,
    that her guests are in the depths of Sheol.

16. **Keep the seventh commandment.**

    **Exodus 20:14** You shall not commit adultery. (NIV)

17. **Anyone who marries a wrongfully divorced person commits
    adultery.**

    **Matthew 5:31–32** It was also said, "Whoever divorces his wife,
    let him give her a certificate of divorce." But I say to you that
    everyone who divorces his wife, except on the ground of sexual
    immorality, makes her commit adultery. And whoever marries
    a divorced woman commits adultery.

18. **Anyone who divorces his or her spouse for any reason other
    than adultery and marries another commits adultery.**

    **Matthew 19:9** And I say to you: whoever divorces his wife,
    except for sexual immorality, and marries another, commits
    adultery.

**Romans 7:2–3** Thus a married woman is bound by law to her husband while he lives, but if her husband dies she is released from the law of marriage. Accordingly, she will be called an adulteress if she lives with another man while her husband is alive. But if her husband dies, she is free from that law, and if she marries another man she is not an adulteress.

19. When he was tempted by Potiphar's wife to commit adultery, Joseph refused to sin against God.

**Genesis 39:6–20**
**Genesis 39:9–10** How then can I do this great wickedness and sin against God? And as she spoke to Joseph day after day, he would not listen to her, to lie beside her or to be with her.

# Affliction, Discipline, Chastisement, Trials

*See also* Comfort, Prayer, Trust

1. **Not all affliction is for specific sins. God often sends affliction to purify and strengthen our faith, for his glory.**

   **1 Peter 1:6–7** In all this you greatly rejoice, though now for a little while you may have had to suffer grief in all kinds of trials. These have come so that the proven genuineness of your faith—of greater worth than gold, which perishes even though refined by fire—may result in praise, glory and honor when Jesus Christ is revealed. (NIV)

   **John 9:1–3** As he went along, he saw a man blind from birth. His disciples asked him, "Rabbi, who sinned, this man or his parents, that he was born blind?" "Neither this man nor his parents sinned," said Jesus, "but this happened so that the works of God might be displayed in him." (NIV)

2. **Job, a godly man, was severely tried; he lost his possessions and his children.**

   **Job 1:1–22**
   **Job 1:1** There was a man in the land of Uz whose name was Job, and that man was blameless and upright, one who feared God and turned away from evil.

   **Job 1:8** And the LORD said to Satan, "Have you considered my servant Job, that there is none like him on the earth, a blameless and upright man, who fears God and turns away from evil?"

3. Job did not get angry at God (which would have been a sinful reaction). Rather, he accepted it by faith and worshiped him.

Job 1:20–22 Then Job arose and tore his robe and shaved his head, and he fell to the ground and worshiped. He said, "Naked I came from my mother's womb, and naked I shall return there. The LORD gave and the LORD has taken away. Blessed be the name of the LORD." Through all this Job did not sin nor did he blame God. (NASB)

4. God at times sends trials to develop patience in us.

James 1:2–4 Consider it all joy, my brethren, when you encounter various trials, knowing that the testing of your faith produces endurance. And let endurance have its perfect result, so that you may be perfect and complete, lacking in nothing. (NASB)

5. The psalmist was thankful for affliction, for it taught him to keep God's precepts.

Psalm 119:67–68 Before I was afflicted I went astray, but now I keep Your word. You are good and do good; teach me Your statutes. (NASB)

Psalm 119:71–72 It is good for me that I was afflicted, that I may learn Your statutes. The law of Your mouth is better to me than thousands of gold and silver pieces. (NASB)

Psalm 119:75–76 I know, O LORD, that Your judgments are righteous, and that in faithfulness You have afflicted me. O may Your lovingkindness comfort me, according to Your word to Your servant. (NASB)

6. We must neither make light of God's discipline nor lose heart because of it.

Hebrews 12:5–6 And have you forgotten the exhortation that addresses you as sons? My son, do not regard lightly the discipline of the Lord, nor be weary when reproved by him. For the Lord disciplines the one he loves, and chastises every son whom he receives.

7. God disciplines his children to promote sanctification.

Hebrews 12:5–11

Hebrews 12:10–11 For our earthly fathers disciplined us for a few years, doing the best they knew how. But God's discipline is always good for us, so that we might share in his holiness. No discipline is enjoyable while it is happening—it's painful! But afterward there will be a peaceful harvest of right living for those who are trained in this way. (NLT)

8. God disciplined and tried his people on their journey to the promised land to teach them important lessons.

Deuteronomy 8:2–5 Remember how the LORD your God led you all the way in the wilderness these forty years, to humble and test you in order to know what was in your heart, whether or not you would keep his commands. He humbled you, causing you to hunger and then feeding you with manna, which neither you nor your ancestors had known, to teach you that man does not live on bread alone but on every word that comes from the mouth of the LORD. Your clothes did not wear out and your feet did not swell during these forty years. Know then in your heart that as a man disciplines his son, so the LORD your God disciplines you. (NIV)

9. God tried his people at Marah, where he turned the bitter water sweet and soon gave a time of refreshment at Elim.

Exodus 15:22–27

Exodus 15:25 Then he cried out to the LORD, and the LORD showed him a tree; and he threw it into the waters, and the waters became sweet. There He made for them a statute and regulation, and there He tested them. (NASB)

Exodus 15:27 Then they came to Elim where there were twelve springs of water and seventy date palms, and they camped there beside the waters. (NASB)

10. To the lukewarm church Jesus declares that he rebukes and disciplines those whom he loves.

Revelation 3:14–22 *(the letter to the church at Laodicea)*

**Revelation 3:19–20** Those whom I love, I reprove and discipline; therefore be zealous and repent. Behold, I stand at the door and knock; if anyone hears My voice and opens the door, I will come in to him and will dine with him, and he with Me. (NASB)

11. **Paul was given a thorn in the flesh, a continual affliction to bear. God promised him that his grace would always be sufficient.**

    **2 Corinthians 12:7–10** Because of the surpassing greatness of the revelations, for this reason, to keep me from exalting myself, there was given me a thorn in the flesh, a messenger of Satan to torment me—to keep me from exalting myself! Concerning this I implored the Lord three times that it might leave me. And He has said to me, "My grace is sufficient for you, for power is perfected in weakness." Most gladly, therefore, I will rather boast about my weaknesses, so that the power of Christ may dwell in me. Therefore I am well content with weaknesses, with insults, with distresses, with persecutions, with difficulties, for Christ's sake; for when I am weak, then I am strong. (NASB)

12. **In everything God works for the good of those who love him.**

    **Romans 8:28** And we know that God causes all things to work together for good to those who love God, to those who are called according to His purpose. (NASB)

13. **God will never give you more than you can bear.**

    **1 Corinthians 10:13** No temptation has overtaken you but such as is common to man; and God is faithful, who will not allow you to be tempted beyond what you are able, but with the temptation will provide the way of escape also, so that you will be able to endure it. (NASB)

14. **We cannot always comprehend God's ways, as he, in his wisdom, carries out his plan.**

    **Romans 11:33–36** Oh, how great are God's riches and wisdom and knowledge! How impossible it is for us to understand his decisions and his ways! For who can know the Lord's thoughts?

Who knows enough to give him advice? And who has given him so much that he needs to pay it back? For everything comes from him and exists by his power and is intended for his glory. All glory to him forever! Amen. (NLT)

15. **King Hezekiah praised God for his loving discipline.**

Isaiah 38:15–19
Isaiah 38:15 But what can I say? He has spoken to me, and he himself has done this. I will walk humbly all my years because of this anguish of my soul. (NIV)
Isaiah 38:17 Surely it was for my benefit that I suffered such anguish. In your love you kept me from the pit of destruction; you have put all my sins behind your back. (NIV)

16. **We can rejoice in our sufferings, which produce perseverance.**

Romans 5:3 More than that, we rejoice in our sufferings, knowing that suffering produces endurance, and endurance produces character, and character produces hope.
James 1:2–4 Count it all joy, my brothers, when you meet trials of various kinds, for you know that the testing of your faith produces steadfastness. And let steadfastness have its full effect, that you may be perfect and complete, lacking in nothing.

17. **God blesses those who persevere under trials.**

James 1:12 Blessed is the man who remains steadfast under trial, for when he has stood the test he will receive the crown of life, which God has promised to those who love him.

18. **Our present sufferings are not worth comparing with the glory that will be revealed in us.**

Romans 8:18 I consider that our present sufferings are not worth comparing with the glory that will be revealed in us. (NIV)

19. Paul says that he suffered under great stress so that he might learn to rely more on God.

2 Corinthians 1:8–9 We do not want you to be uninformed, brothers and sisters, about the troubles we experienced in the province of Asia. We were under great pressure, far beyond our ability to endure, so that we despaired of life itself. Indeed, we felt we had received the sentence of death. But this happened that we might not rely on ourselves but on God, who raises the dead. (NIV)

20. Paul says that God always has and always will deliver him.

2 Corinthians 1:10–11 He has delivered us from such a deadly peril, and he will deliver us again. On him we have set our hope that he will continue to deliver us, as you help us by your prayers. Then many will give thanks on our behalf for the gracious favor granted us in answer to the prayers of many. (NIV)

21. At times God gives us trials so that our faith may be purified as gold is refined by fire, that Christ may be honored and glorified.

1 Peter 1:7–8 These trials will show that your faith is genuine. It is being tested as fire tests and purifies gold—though your faith is far more precious than mere gold. So when your faith remains strong through many trials, it will bring you much praise and glory and honor on the day when Jesus Christ is revealed to the whole world. You love him even though you have never seen him. Though you do not see him now, you trust him; and you rejoice with a glorious, inexpressible joy. (NLT)

22. In the time of trouble you can experience God's protective care and, even through the tears, sing praises to God.

Psalm 27:5–6 For he will hide me in his shelter in the day of trouble; he will conceal me under the cover of his tent; he will lift me high upon a rock. And now my head shall be lifted up above my enemies all around me, and I will offer in his tent sacrifices with shouts of joy; I will sing and make melody to the Lord.

23. Paul and Silas were singing praises to God while they were suffering severely for the sake of the gospel.

Acts 16:16–28 *(Paul and Silas were severely flogged, thrown into prison, and their feet were fastened in stocks.)*

Acts 16:25 About midnight Paul and Silas were praying and singing hymns to God, and the other prisoners were listening to them. (NIV)

24. While he was suffering in prison at Rome, Paul rejoiced over what God was accomplishing through it all.

Philippians 1:12–26

Philippians 1:12–14 Now I want you to know, brethren, that my circumstances have turned out for the greater progress of the gospel, so that my imprisonment in the cause of Christ has become well known throughout the whole praetorian guard and to everyone else, and that most of the brethren, trusting in the Lord because of my imprisonment, have far more courage to speak the word of God without fear. (NASB)

25. Although Paul suffered in many ways, he did not lose heart. God kept strengthening him day by day, and he looked forward to his eternal reward.

2 Corinthians 4:8–18

2 Corinthians 4:16–18 Therefore we do not lose heart. Though outwardly we are wasting away, yet inwardly we are being renewed day by day. For our light and momentary troubles are achieving for us an eternal glory that far outweighs them all. So we fix our eyes not on what is seen, but on what is unseen, since what is seen is temporary, but what is unseen is eternal. (NIV)

For more on how to handle affliction, see Death, Eternal Life, Providence of God.

# Alcohol, Drug Abuse

*See also* Overcoming Sin

1. **Your body is a temple of the Holy Spirit.**

   **1 Corinthians 6:15** Do you not know that your bodies are members of Christ? Shall I then take the members of Christ and make them members of a prostitute? Never!

   **1 Corinthians 6:19–20** Or do you not know that your body is a temple of the Holy Spirit within you, whom you have from God? You are not your own, for you were bought with a price. So glorify God in your body.

2. **Jesus warns against the abuse of alcohol.**

   **Luke 21:34** But watch yourselves lest your hearts be weighed down with dissipation and drunkenness and cares of this life, and that day come upon you suddenly like a trap.

3. **Wine is a mocker, beer a brawler.**

   **Proverbs 20:1** Wine is a mocker, strong drink a brawler, and whoever is led astray by it is not wise.

4. **Don't love wine.**

   **Proverbs 21:17** Whoever loves pleasure will be a poor man; he who loves wine and oil will not be rich.

5. **Heavy drinking brings misery.**

   **Proverbs 23:29–35**

6. Consider the sad picture of a drunkard. (The Bible tells it like it is!)

> Proverbs 23:32–35

7. God's wrath was upon Israel for its sin of drunkenness.

> Isaiah 28:1–4

8. Isaiah gives us a vivid picture of a drunk losing his moral judgment.

> Isaiah 28:7–8 These also stagger from wine and reel from beer: Priests and prophets stagger from beer and are befuddled with wine; they reel from beer, they stagger when seeing visions, they stumble when rendering decisions. All the tables are covered with vomit and there is not a spot without filth. (NIV)

9. Paul gives us a timely warning and instruction.

> Ephesians 5:15–18 Be very careful, then, how you live—not as unwise but as wise, making the most of every opportunity, because the days are evil. Therefore do not be foolish, but understand what the Lord's will is. Do not get drunk on wine, which leads to debauchery. Instead, be filled with the Spirit. (NIV)

10. Drunkenness breaks down morals.

> Genesis 9:20–23 *(the example of Noah)*
> Genesis 19:30–38 *(the example of Lot)*

11. No drunkard shall enter heaven.

> 1 Corinthians 6:9–10 Do you not know that the unrighteous will not inherit the kingdom of God? Do not be deceived: neither the sexually immoral . . . nor drunkards . . . will inherit the kingdom of God.

12. One can be saved from drunkenness and set free.

> 1 Corinthians 6:11 And such were some of you [drunkards, etc.]. But you were washed, you were sanctified, you were justified in the name of the Lord Jesus Christ and by the Spirit of our God.

13. **Don't associate with drunkards.**

1 Corinthians 5:11 But now I am writing to you not to associate with anyone who bears the name of brother if he is guilty of sexual immorality or greed, or is an idolater, reviler, drunkard, or swindler—not even to eat with such a one.

14. **Be wise! Don't join those who abuse alcohol.**

Proverbs 23:19–20 Listen, my son, and be wise, and set your heart on the right path: Do not join those who drink too much wine or gorge themselves on meat. (NIV)

# Anger, Hot Temper

*For help* in overcoming uncontrolled anger and a hot temper, see also Overcoming Sin, Progressive Sanctification, Self-Control

1. **Anger is not in itself sinful.**

    **Psalm 7:11** *(God is angry with the wicked.)*
    **1 Kings 11:9** *(God was angry with Solomon.)*
    **2 Kings 17:18** *(God was angry with Israel.)*
    **Mark 3:5** *(Jesus was angry with the Pharisees.)*

2. **Be slow to become angry.**

    **Proverbs 14:16–17** The wise are cautious and avoid danger; fools plunge ahead with reckless confidence. Short-tempered people do foolish things, and schemers are hated. (NLT)
    **Proverbs 14:29** People with understanding control their anger; a hot temper shows great foolishness. (NLT)
    **James 1:19–20** Know this, my beloved brothers: let every person be quick to hear, slow to speak, slow to anger; for the anger of man does not produce the righteousness that God requires.

3. **Love covers a multitude of sins and overlooks many offenses.**

    **Proverbs 10:12** Hatred stirs up quarrels, but love makes up for all offenses. (NLT)
    **Proverbs 12:16** A fool is quick-tempered, but a wise person stays calm when insulted. (NLT)
    **Proverbs 17:9** Love prospers when a fault is forgiven, but dwelling on it separates close friends. (NLT)
    **Proverbs 19:11** Sensible people control their temper; they earn respect by overlooking wrongs. (NLT)
    **1 Peter 4:8** Above all, keep loving one another earnestly, since love covers a multitude of sins.

4. **Seek the way of love.**

   **1 Corinthians 13:4–5** Love is patient, love is kind. . . . it is not easily angered. (NIV)

5. **Cain's anger turned into hate and murder.**

   **Genesis 4:3–8**
   **Genesis 4:4** And Abel also brought an offering—fat portions from some of the firstborn of his flock. The LORD looked with favor on Abel and his offering.
   **Genesis 4:8** Now Cain said to his brother Abel, "Let's go out to the field." While they were in the field, Cain attacked his brother Abel and killed him. (NIV)

6. **Hot words stir up strife.**

   **Proverbs 15:1** A soft answer turns away wrath, but a harsh word stirs up anger. (NKJV)

7. **A hot-tempered man creates dissension.**

   **Proverbs 15:18** A hot-tempered man stirs up strife, but the slow to anger calms a dispute. (NASB)

8. **Do not associate with a hot-tempered man.**

   **Proverbs 22:24–25** Do not make friends with a hot-tempered person, do not associate with one easily angered, or you may learn their ways and get yourself ensnared. (NIV)

9. **Control yourself.**

   **Proverbs 25:28** A man without self-control is like a city broken into and left without walls.
   **Proverbs 29:22** A man of wrath stirs up strife, and one given to anger causes much transgression.
   **Proverbs 30:33** Pressing milk produces curds, pressing the nose produces blood, and pressing anger produces strife.

10. **Fits of rage belong to your sinful nature, the way of sin.**
    **Galatians 5:19–21**

11. **Good news! Through the Spirit you can overcome the sin of a hot temper.**

    **Galatians 5:22–25** But the fruit of the Spirit is love, joy, peace, patience, kindness, goodness, faithfulness, gentleness, self-control; against such things there is no law. And those who belong to Christ Jesus have crucified the flesh with its passions and desires. If we live by the Spirit, let us also walk by the Spirit.

    **Colossians 3:8** But now you must put them all away: anger, wrath, malice, slander, and obscene talk from your mouth.

12. **Handle anger in a godly way. Do not let the sun go down on your anger.**

    **Ephesians 4:26** "In your anger do not sin": Do not let the sun go down while you are still angry. (NIV)

13. **Jesus said that one who is angry with his brother without a cause will be subject to judgment.**

    **Matthew 5:21–22** You have heard that it was said to those of old, "You shall not murder; and whoever murders will be liable to judgment." But I say to you that everyone who is angry with his brother will be liable to judgment; whoever insults his brother will be liable to the council; and whoever says, "You fool!" will be liable to the hell of fire.

# Assurance (of Salvation)

### 1. Job had assurance.

Job 19:25–27 But as for me, I know that my Redeemer lives, and he will stand upon the earth at last. And after my body has decayed, yet in my body I will see God! I will see him for myself. Yes, I will see him with my own eyes. I am overwhelmed at the thought! (NLT)

### 2. The Spirit testifies with our spirit.

Romans 8:16–17 For his Spirit joins with our spirit to affirm that we are God's children. And since we are his children, we are his heirs. In fact, together with Christ we are heirs of God's glory. But if we are to share his glory, we must also share his suffering. (NLT)

### 3. We know that we live in him; we know and rely on the love God has for us.

1 John 4:13–16 And God has given us his Spirit as proof that we live in him and he in us. Furthermore, we have seen with our own eyes and now testify that the Father sent his Son to be the Savior of the world. All who confess that Jesus is the Son of God have God living in them, and they live in God. We know how much God loves us, and we have put our trust in his love. (NLT)

### 4. You may know that you have eternal life.

1 John 5:13 I have written this to you who believe in the name of the Son of God, so that you may know you have eternal life. (NLT)

**5. Paul had assurance of eternal life.**

**2 Timothy 1:12** I know whom I have believed and I am convinced that He is able to guard what I have entrusted to Him until that day. (NASB)

**6. Now we are the children of God, and we shall be like him.**

**1 John 3:1–3** See how great a love the Father has bestowed on us, that we would be called children of God; and such we are. For this reason the world does not know us, because it did not know Him. Beloved, now we are children of God, and it has not appeared as yet what we will be. We know that when He appears, we will be like Him, because we will see Him just as He is. And everyone who has this hope fixed on Him purifies himself, just as He is pure. (NASB)

**7. A Christian has a living hope through Christ's resurrection.**

**1 Peter 1:3–5** Blessed be the God and Father of our Lord Jesus Christ, who according to His great mercy has caused us to be born again to a living hope through the resurrection of Jesus Christ from the dead, to obtain an inheritance which is imperishable and undefiled and will not fade away, reserved in heaven for you, who are protected by the power of God through faith for a salvation ready to be revealed in the last time. (NASB)

# Bitterness, Resentment, Hate

1. In the power of the Holy Spirit every Christian can and must get rid of bitterness and hatred and become a kind, compassionate, forgiving person.

   Ephesians 4:31–32 Get rid of all bitterness, rage and anger, brawling and slander, along with every form of malice. Be kind and compassionate to one another, forgiving each other, just as in Christ God forgave you. (NIV)

2. Quit biting and devouring each other.

   Galatians 5:15 If you bite and devour each other, watch out or you will be destroyed by each other. (NIV)

3. Bitterness belongs to the sinful nature.

   Galatians 5:19 The acts of the flesh are obvious: sexual immorality, impurity and debauchery. (NIV)

4. Let no bitter root grow.

   Hebrews 12:15 See to it that no one falls short of the grace of God and that no bitter root grows up to cause trouble and defile many. (NIV)

5. Joseph's brothers allowed bitterness to grow into hatred and murder in the heart.

   Genesis 37

6. Cain's anger turned to bitterness, hatred, and murder.

   Genesis 4:3–8

7. **Hatred is forbidden.**

Leviticus 19:16–17 You shall not go about as a slanderer among your people, and you are not to act against the life of your neighbor; I am the LORD. You shall not hate your fellow countryman in your heart; you may surely reprove your neighbor, but shall not incur sin because of him. (NASB)

8. **One who hates lives in darkness.**

1 John 2:9–11 Whoever says he is in the light and hates his brother is still in darkness. Whoever loves his brother abides in the light, and in him there is no cause for stumbling. But whoever hates his brother is in the darkness and walks in the darkness, and does not know where he is going, because the darkness has blinded his eyes.

9. **The way of a malicious man is deceitful.**

Proverbs 26:24–26 Enemies disguise themselves with their lips, but in their hearts they harbor deceit. Though their speech is charming, do not believe them, for seven abominations fill their hearts. Their malice may be concealed by deception, but their wickedness will be exposed in the assembly. (NIV)

10. **Hatred is murder.**

1 John 3:11–20
1 John 3:15 Anyone who hates a brother or sister is a murderer, and you know that no murderer has eternal life residing in him. (NIV)

11. **Jesus commands us not to hate our enemies, but love them and pray for them.**

Matthew 5:43–48

12. **If you claim to love God but you hate your brother, you are a liar.**

1 John 4:20–21 If anyone says, "I love God," and hates his brother, he is a liar; for he who does not love his brother whom

he has seen cannot love God whom he has not seen. And this commandment we have from him: whoever loves God must also love his brother.

13. **To conceal or harbor hatred in your heart is lying before the face of God.**

    **Proverbs 10:18** The one who conceals hatred has lying lips, and whoever utters slander is a fool.

14. **Hatred stirs up dissension.**

    **Proverbs 10:12** Hatred stirs up strife, but love covers all offenses.

# Blame Shifting

**1. Adam and Eve tried to shift blame.**

Genesis 3:12–13 Then the man said, "The woman whom You gave to be with me, she gave me of the tree, and I ate." And the Lord God said to the woman, "What is this you have done?" The woman said, "The serpent deceived me, and I ate." (NKJV)

**2. Some try to blame God.**

Proverbs 19:3 The foolishness of a man twists his way, and his heart frets against the Lord. (NKJV)

**3. Do not judge others while you fail to acknowledge your own sin.**

Matthew 7:1–5 Judge not, that you be not judged. For with what judgment you judge, you will be judged; and with the measure you use, it will be measured back to you. And why do you look at the speck in your brother's eye, but do not consider the plank in your own eye? Or how can you say to your brother, "Let me remove the speck from your eye"; and look, a plank is in your own eye? Hypocrite! First remove the plank from your own eye, and then you will see clearly to remove the speck from your brother's eye. (NKJV)

# Children

*See also* Training Children, Youth

**1. Children belong first to God and are his gift to us.**

Psalm 127:3–5
Psalm 127:3 Children are a heritage from the LORD, offspring a reward from him. (NIV)

**2. Children of believers belong to God and are in his covenant.**

Genesis 17:7 I will establish my covenant as an everlasting covenant between me and you and your descendants after you for the generations to come, to be your God and the God of your descendants after you. (NIV)

Acts 2:39 The promise is for you and your children and for all who are far off—for all whom the Lord our God will call. (NIV)

**3. God delights in the praise and worship of children.**

Psalm 8:2 Out of the mouth of babes and infants, you have established strength because of your foes, to still the enemy and the avenger.

**4. Jesus accepted the praise of children.**

Matthew 21:15–16 But when the chief priests and the scribes saw the wonderful things that he did, and the children crying out in the temple, "Hosanna to the Son of David!" they were indignant, and they said to him, "Do you hear what these are saying?" And Jesus said to them, "Yes; have you never read, 'Out of the mouth of infants and nursing babies you have prepared praise'?"

5. Jesus loves little children; of such is God's kingdom.

Matthew 19:13–15 Then children were brought to him that he might lay his hands on them and pray. The disciples rebuked the people, but Jesus said, "Let the little children come to me and do not hinder them, for to such belongs the kingdom of heaven." And he laid his hands on them and went away.

6. David was comforted by the knowledge that his infant son went to heaven when he died and that he would see him there.

2 Samuel 12:18–23
2 Samuel 12:23 But now he is dead. Why should I fast? Can I bring him back again? I shall go to him, but he will not return to me.

# Church, Communion of Saints

*See also* Loving and Serving Others, Church Discipline

1. **The church is one.**

   **Ephesians 4:3–6** Make every effort to keep yourselves united in the Spirit, binding yourselves together with peace. For there is one body and one Spirit, just as you have been called to one glorious hope for the future. There is one Lord, one faith, one baptism, and one God and Father, who is over all and in all and living through all. (NLT)

2. **The church is one body with many functions; each member has a purpose.**

   **Romans 12:4–8** Just as our bodies have many parts and each part has a special function, so it is with Christ's body. We are many parts of one body, and we all belong to each other. In his grace, God has given us different gifts for doing certain things well. So if God has given you the ability to prophesy, speak out with as much faith as God has given you. If your gift is serving others, serve them well. If you are a teacher, teach well. If your gift is to encourage others, be encouraging. If it is giving, give generously. If God has given you leadership ability, take the responsibility seriously. And if you have a gift for showing kindness to others, do it gladly. (NLT)

3. **Together, Christians constitute God's household, in which he lives by his Spirit.**

   **Ephesians 2:19–22** So now you Gentiles are no longer strangers and foreigners. You are citizens along with all of God's holy people. You are members of God's family. Together, we are his house, built on the foundation of the apostles and the prophets.

And the cornerstone is Christ Jesus himself. We are carefully joined together in him, becoming a holy temple for the Lord. Through him you Gentiles are also being made part of this dwelling where God lives by his Spirit. (NLT)

4. **Keep the unity of believers; don't follow men, but Christ.**

   1 Corinthians 1:10–17
   1 Corinthians 1:11–13 For it has been reported to me by Chloe's people that there is quarreling among you, my brothers. What I mean is that each one of you says, "I follow Paul," or "I follow Apollos," or "I follow Cephas," or "I follow Christ." Is Christ divided? Was Paul crucified for you? Or were you baptized in the name of Paul?

5. **Gifts of the Spirit differ. Each member must use his or her gifts to serve others.**

   Ephesians 4:11–13 And He gave some as apostles, and some as prophets, and some as evangelists, and some as pastors and teachers, for the equipping of the saints for the work of service, to the building up of the body of Christ; until we all attain to the unity of the faith, and of the knowledge of the Son of God, to a mature man, to the measure of the stature which belongs to the fullness of Christ. (NASB)
   1 Corinthians 12:1–11
   1 Corinthians 12:4–7 Now there are varieties of gifts, but the same Spirit; and there are varieties of service, but the same Lord; and there are varieties of activities, but it is the same God who empowers them all in everyone. To each is given the manifestation of the Spirit for the common good.

6. **Each member of the body is necessary. We need one another. All must have a deep concern for each other.**

   1 Corinthians 12:12–31
   1 Corinthians 12:25–26 . . . so that there may be no division in the body, but that the members may have the same care for one another. And if one member suffers, all the members suffer

with it; if one member is honored, all the members rejoice with it. (NASB)

7. **Christ is the head of the church, his body.**

**Ephesians 1:20–23**
**Ephesians 1:22–23** And God placed all things under his feet and appointed him to be head over everything for the church, which is his body, the fullness of him who fills everything in every way. (NIV)
**Ephesians 5:23** For the husband is the head of the wife as Christ is the head of the church, his body, of which he is the Savior. (NIV)

8. **Christ loves the church.**

**Ephesians 5:25** Husbands, love your wives, just as Christ loved the church and gave himself up for her. (NIV)

9. **Attend worship services faithfully.**

**Hebrews 10:25** And let us not neglect our meeting together, as some people do, but encourage one another, especially now that the day of his return is drawing near. (NLT)

10. **The psalmist longed to be in the house of God.**

**Psalm 84**
**Psalm 84:1–2** How lovely is your dwelling place, O LORD of hosts! My soul longs, yes, faints for the courts of the LORD; my heart and flesh sing for joy to the living God.
**Psalm 84:10** For a day in your courts is better than a thousand elsewhere. I would rather be a doorkeeper in the house of my God than dwell in the tents of wickedness.

11. **The meaning of the communion of the saints is beautifully taught in Paul's letter to Philemon.**

**The book of Philemon** (*Paul writes the letter to his "dear friend and fellow worker" on behalf of Onesimus, urging Philemon to receive him back as a "dear brother."*)

Verses 10–12 I appeal to you for my son Onesimus, who became my son while I was in chains. Formerly he was useless to you, but now he has become useful both to you and to me. I am sending him—who is my very heart—back to you. (NIV)

Verses 15–16 Perhaps the reason he was separated from you for a little while was that you might have him back forever—no longer as a slave, but better than a slave, as a dear brother. He is very dear to me but even dearer to you, both as a fellow man and as a brother in the Lord. (NIV)

12. **Elders are God's appointed shepherds placed over the flock of Jesus Christ.**

Acts 20:28 Pay careful attention to yourselves and to all the flock, in which the Holy Spirit has made you overseers, to care for the church of God, which he obtained with his own blood.

13. **Office bearers must warn the wayward.**

Ezekiel 33:7–9 So you, son of man, I have made a watchman for the house of Israel. Whenever you hear a word from my mouth, you shall give them warning from me. If I say to the wicked, O wicked one, you shall surely die, and you do not speak to warn the wicked to turn from his way, that wicked person shall die in his iniquity, but his blood I will require at your hand. But if you warn the wicked to turn from his way, and he does not turn from his way, that person shall die in his iniquity, but you will have delivered your soul.

14. **God condemns and warns unfaithful shepherds.**

   **Ezekiel 34:1–16**

15. **Members of the church must honor and obey the elders whom God has appointed to exercise authority in the church.**

1 Timothy 5:17 Let the elders who rule well be considered worthy of double honor, especially those who labor in preaching and teaching.

Hebrews 13:17 Obey your leaders and submit to them, for they are keeping watch over your souls, as those who will have to give an account. Let them do this with joy and not with groaning, for that would be of no advantage to you.

16. **God's office bearers must say all and only that which he requires of them, even when they are under great pressure to do otherwise.**

    **1 Kings 22:1–14**

    **1 Kings 22:8–9** So the king of Israel said to Jehoshaphat (king of Judah), "There is still one man, Micaiah the son of Imlah, by whom we may inquire of the LORD; but I hate him, because he does not prophesy good concerning me, but evil." And Jehoshaphat said, "Let not the king say such things!" Then the king of Israel called an officer and said, "Bring Micaiah the son of Imlah quickly!" (NKJV)

    **1 Kings 22:13–14** Then the messenger who had gone to call Micaiah spoke to him, saying, "Now listen, the words of the prophets with one accord encourage the king. Please, let your word be like the word of one of them, and speak encouragement." And Micaiah said, "As the LORD lives, whatever the LORD says to me, that I will speak." (NKJV)

17. **Jesus prays for the church.**

    **John 17:6–26** *(Jesus' high priestly prayer)*

18. **The church is a great multitude gathered from all nations and tribes.**

    **Revelation 7:9** After these things I looked, and behold, a great multitude which no one could count, from every nation and all tribes and peoples and tongues, standing before the throne and before the Lamb, clothed in white robes, and palm branches were in their hands. (NASB)

# Church Discipline

**1. Discipline begins with personal admonition.**

**Romans 15:14** I myself am convinced, my brothers and sisters, that you yourselves are full of goodness, filled with knowledge and competent to instruct one another. (NIV)

**Colossians 3:16** Let the message of Christ dwell among you richly as you teach and admonish one another with all wisdom through psalms, hymns, and songs from the Spirit, singing to God with gratitude in your hearts. (NIV)

**2. Restore one who has fallen, with gentleness.**

**Galatians 6:1** Brothers, if anyone is caught in any transgression, you who are spiritual should restore him in a spirit of gentleness. Keep watch on yourself, lest you too be tempted.

**3. Seek to save an erring sinner.**

**James 5:19–20** My brothers, if anyone among you wanders from the truth and someone brings him back, let him know that whoever brings back a sinner from his wandering will save his soul from death and will cover a multitude of sins.

**4. Forgive and restore one who repents; love him.**

**2 Corinthians 2:7–8** Now, however, it is time to forgive and comfort him. Otherwise he may be overcome by discouragement. So I urge you now to reaffirm your love for him. (NLT)

**5. Do not fellowship with one who will not repent.**

**1 Corinthians 5:11** Now I am writing to you not to associate with anyone who bears the name of brother if he is guilty of sexual immorality or greed, or is an idolater, reviler, drunkard, or swindler—not even to eat with such a one.

6. **Jesus gives us the procedure for church discipline.**

**Matthew 18:15–18** If your brother sins against you, go and tell him his fault, between you and him alone. If he listens to you, you have gained your brother. But if he does not listen, take one or two others along with you, that every charge may be established by the evidence of two or three witnesses. If he refuses to listen to them, tell it to the church. And if he refuses to listen even to the church, let him be to you as a Gentile and a tax collector. Truly, I say to you, whatever you bind on earth shall be bound in heaven, and whatever you loose on earth shall be loosed in heaven.

7. **Christ has given the keys of the kingdom to the church.**

**Matthew 16:19** I will give you the keys of the kingdom of heaven, and whatever you bind on earth shall be bound in heaven, and whatever you loose on earth shall be loosed in heaven. Then he strictly charged the disciples to tell no one that he was the Christ.

8. **Purge out the old leaven.**

**1 Corinthians 5:1–13**

9. **Excommunication is sometimes necessary.**

**2 Thessalonians 3:14** If anyone does not obey our instruction in this letter, take special note of that person and do not associate with him, so that he will be put to shame. Yet do not regard him as an enemy, but admonish him as a brother. (NASB)

10. **Jesus commends the church for faithful discipline.**

**Revelation 2:2** I know all the things you do. I have seen your hard work and your patient endurance. I know you don't tolerate evil people. You have examined the claims of those who say they are apostles but are not. You have discovered they are liars. (NLT)

11. **Jesus rebukes the church that does not discipline.**

**Revelation 2:14–16** But I have a few complaints against you. You tolerate some among you whose teaching is like that of Balaam, who showed Balak how to trip up the people of Israel. He taught them to sin by eating food offered to idols and by committing sexual sin. In a similar way, you have some Nicolaitans among you who follow the same teaching. Repent of your sin, or I will come to you suddenly and fight against them with the sword of my mouth. (NLT)

# Comfort

*See also* Death, Forgiveness of Sins, Prayer, Providence of God, Trust

1. The Lord is our shepherd, always leading us in the best way and protecting us.

   Psalm 23

2. As an eagle stirs up its nest and hovers over its young, so God cares for his own.

   Deuteronomy 32:10–12 He encircled him, He instructed him, He kept him as the apple of His eye. As an eagle stirs up its nest, hovers over its young, spreading out its wings, taking them up, carrying them on its wings, so the Lord alone led him, and there was no foreign god with him. (NKJV)

3. As a father cares for his children, so God cares for his own; his love is everlasting.

   Psalm 103:8–18

4. God always shelters those who put their trust in him.

   Psalm 91:1–2 He who dwells in the shelter of the Most High will abide in the shadow of the Almighty. I will say to the LORD, "My refuge and my fortress, my God, in whom I trust!" (NASB)

5. God knows us most intimately; he holds and guides us by his hand.

   Psalm 139:1–12
   Psalm 139:1–3 O LORD, you have searched me and known me. You know when I sit down and when I rise up; You understand

my thought from afar. You scrutinize my path and my lying down, and are intimately acquainted with all my ways. (NASB)

Psalm 139:9–10 If I take the wings of the dawn, if I dwell in the remotest part of the sea, even there Your hand will lead me, and Your right hand will lay hold of me. (NASB)

6. The wicked appear to prosper for a time, while the righteous suffer; but actually God is always leading us in the best way; he comforts us with his presence.

Psalm 73
Psalm 73:23–24 Yet I am always with you; you hold me by my right hand. You guide me with your counsel, and afterward you will take me into glory. (NIV)

7. The sufferings of the present time are not worth comparing with the coming glory.

Romans 8:18 For I consider that the sufferings of this present time are not worthy to be compared with the glory that is to be revealed to us. (NASB)

8. God works all things together for our good.

Romans 8:28 And we know that God causes all things to work together for good to those who love God, to those who are called according to His purpose. (NASB)

9. If God is for us, nothing can separate us from his love.

Romans 8:31–39
Romans 8:31 What then shall we say to these things? If God is for us, who can be against us?

Romans 8:38–39 For I am sure that neither death nor life, nor angels nor rulers, nor things present nor things to come, nor powers, nor height nor depth, nor anything else in all creation, will be able to separate us from the love of God in Christ Jesus our Lord.

10. Jesus, the good shepherd, died for his sheep; he knows, leads, and protects each one; he gives us eternal security.

John 10:11 I am the good shepherd. The good shepherd lays down his life for the sheep.

John 10:14–15 I am the good shepherd. I know my own and my own know me, just as the Father knows me and I know the Father; and I lay down my life for the sheep.

John 10:27–29 My sheep hear my voice, and I know them, and they follow me. I give them eternal life, and they will never perish, and no one will snatch them out of my hand. My Father, who has given them to me, is greater than all, and no one is able to snatch them out of the Father's hand.

11. God's grace is sufficient for every need.

2 Corinthians 9:8 And God is able to make all grace abound to you, so that having all sufficiency in all things at all times, you may abound in every good work.

12. Paul had a thorn in the flesh; God's promise: My grace is sufficient for you.

2 Corinthians 12:7–10

2 Corinthians 12:9 But he said to me, "My grace is sufficient for you, for my power is made perfect in weakness." Therefore I will boast all the more gladly of my weaknesses, so that the power of Christ may rest upon me.

13. Jesus rebuked the disciples for their little faith and calmed the storm.

Matthew 8:23–27

14. God directs all things by his infinite wisdom and his ways are beyond tracing out.

Romans 11:33–36 Oh, how great are God's riches and wisdom and knowledge! How impossible it is for us to understand his decisions and his ways! For who can know the Lord's thoughts? Who knows enough to give him advice? And who has given him so much that he needs to pay it back? For everything comes from him and exists by his power and is intended for his glory. All glory to him forever! Amen. (NLT)

15. **One day this life of suffering will be over and all will be made new.**

Revelation 21:1–4
Revelation 21:3–4 And I heard a loud voice from the throne, saying, "Behold, the tabernacle of God is among men, and He will dwell among them, and they shall be His people, and God Himself will be among them, and He will wipe away every tear from their eyes; and there will no longer be any death; there will no longer be any mourning, or crying, or pain; the first things have passed away." (NASB)

16. **Cast your concerns on the Lord, for he will support you.**

Psalm 55:22 Cast your burden upon the Lord and He will sustain you; He will never allow the righteous to be shaken. (NASB)

17. **God is the source of all comfort.**

2 Corinthians 1:3–4 Blessed be the God and Father of our Lord Jesus Christ, the Father of mercies and God of all comfort, who comforts us in all our affliction so that we will be able to comfort those who are in any affliction with the comfort with which we ourselves are comforted by God. (NASB)

18. **God is unchangeably faithful.**

Psalm 89:1–8
Psalm 89:1–2 I will sing of the Lord's great love forever; with my mouth I will make your faithfulness known through all generations. I will declare that your love stands firm forever, that you established your faithfulness in heaven itself. (NIV)
Psalm 89:8 O Lord God Almighty, who is like you? You are mighty, O Lord, and your faithfulness surrounds you. (NIV)

19. The Lord tends his flock like a shepherd.

Isaiah 40:10–11 Yes, the Sovereign LORD is coming in power. He will rule with a powerful arm. See, he brings his reward with him as he comes. He will feed his flock like a shepherd. He will carry the lambs in his arms, holding them close to his heart. He will gently lead the mother sheep with their young. (NLT)

20. God's favor lasts for a lifetime. He turns weeping into rejoicing.

Psalm 30:4–5 Sing to the LORD, all you godly ones! Praise his holy name. For his anger lasts only a moment, but his favor lasts a lifetime! Weeping may last through the night, but joy comes with the morning. (NLT)

21. God has made a commitment to supply all your actual needs.

Philippians 4:19 And my God will meet all your needs according to his glorious riches in Christ Jesus. (NIV)

# Communication, Gossip, Lying

1. **The psalmist has given us a model prayer for good speech.**

   **Psalm 19:14** Let the words of my mouth and the meditation of my heart be acceptable in Your sight, O LORD, my strength and my Redeemer. (NKJV)

   **Psalm 141:3** Set a guard, O LORD, over my mouth; keep watch over the door of my lips. (NKJV)

2. **Commit yourself to speaking only what is right and true.**

   **Proverbs 8:6–8** Listen, for I will speak of excellent things, and from the opening of my lips will come right things; for my mouth will speak truth; wickedness is an abomination to my lips. All the words of my mouth are with righteousness; nothing crooked or perverse is in them. (NKJV)

3. **Speak the truth in love, not harshly.**

   **Ephesians 4:15** Rather, speaking the truth in love, we are to grow up in every way into him who is the head, into Christ.

   **Ephesians 4:29** Let no corrupting talk come out of your mouths, but only such as is good for building up, as fits the occasion, that it may give grace to those who hear.

4. **Avoid harsh words.**

   **Proverbs 15:1** A soft answer turns away wrath, but a harsh word stirs up anger.

5. **Be quick to listen, slow to speak.**

   **James 1:19** Understand this, my dear brothers and sisters: You must all be quick to listen, slow to speak, and slow to get angry. (NLT)

51

Ecclesiastes 5:3–5 For a dream comes through much activity, and a fool's voice is known by his many words. When you make a vow to God, do not delay to pay it; for He has no pleasure in fools. Pay what you have vowed—better not to vow than to vow and not pay. (NKJV)

Proverbs 10:19 When there are many words, transgression is unavoidable, but he who restrains his lips is wise. (NASB)

Proverbs 15:28 The heart of the righteous ponders how to answer, but the mouth of the wicked pours out evil things. (NASB)

Proverbs 17:28 Even a fool, when he keeps silent, is considered wise; when he closes his lips, he is considered prudent. (NASB)

### 6. Listen before you speak.

Proverbs 18:13 He who answers a matter before he hears it, it is folly and shame to him. (NKJV)

Proverbs 29:20 Do you see a man hasty in his words? There is more hope for a fool than for him. (NKJV)

### 7. God forbids us to lie; he wants us to speak the truth.

Exodus 20:16 You shall not bear false witness against your neighbor. (NASB)

Ephesians 4:25 Therefore, laying aside falsehood, speak truth each one of you with his neighbor for we are members of one another. (NASB)

### 8. The Lord detests lying.

Proverbs 12:22 The LORD detests lying lips, but he delights in those who tell the truth. (NLT)

Psalm 34:11–14 Come, my children, and listen to me, and I will teach you to fear the LORD. Does anyone want to live a life that is long and prosperous? Then keep your tongue from speaking evil and your lips from telling lies! Turn away from evil and do good. Search for peace, and work to maintain it. (NLT)

9. All lying is of the devil, the father of all lies.

John 8:44 There is no truth in [the devil]. When he lies, he speaks his native language, for he is a liar and the father of lies. (NIV)

10. Lying will be punished.

Proverbs 19:9 A false witness will not go unpunished, and whoever pours out lies will perish. (NIV)

11. Do not hurt your neighbor by gossip or careless talk; control your tongue.

Proverbs 11:11–13 By the blessing of the upright a city is exalted, but by the mouth of the wicked it is overthrown. Whoever belittles his neighbor lacks sense, but a man of understanding remains silent. Whoever goes about slandering reveals secrets, but he who is trustworthy in spirit keeps a thing covered.

Proverbs 12:18 There is one whose rash words are like sword thrusts, but the tongue of the wise brings healing.

Proverbs 17:27–28 Whoever restrains his words has knowledge, and he who has a cool spirit is a man of understanding. Even a fool who keeps silent is considered wise; when he closes his lips, he is deemed intelligent.

Proverbs 29:19 By mere words a servant is not disciplined, for though he understands, he will not respond.

Proverbs 21:23 Whoever keeps his mouth and his tongue keeps himself out of trouble.

12. Tame the tongue; it can be very destructive.

James 3:1–12

13. We must help stop gossip and strife.

Proverbs 16:20 He who heeds the word wisely will find good, and whoever trusts in the LORD, happy is he. (NKJV)

14. **Be careful. Don't speak rashly.**

> **Proverbs 13:3** Those who control their tongue will have a long life; opening your mouth can ruin everything. (NLT)

15. **A word aptly spoken and a wise rebuke can be very helpful to others.**

> **Proverbs 25:11–12** Like apples of gold in settings of silver is a word spoken in right circumstances. Like an earring of gold and an ornament of fine gold is a wise reprover to a listening ear. (NASB)
>
> **Proverbs 15:4** A soothing tongue is a tree of life, but perversion in it crushes the spirit. (NASB)

# Conscience

### 1. Keep a clear conscience.

1 Peter 3:15–16 In your hearts revere Christ as Lord. Always be prepared to give an answer to everyone who asks you to give the reason for the hope that you have. But do this with gentleness and respect, keeping a clear conscience, so that those who speak maliciously against your good behavior in Christ may be ashamed of their slander. (NIV)

### 2. Keep a clear conscience before God and men.

Acts 24:16 So I always take pains to have a clear conscience toward both God and man.

### 3. Hold to the truths of the faith.

1 Timothy 3:9 They must be committed to the mystery of the faith now revealed and must live with a clear conscience. (NLT)

### 4. A conscience can be seared.

1 Timothy 4:2 These people are hypocrites and liars, and their consciences are dead. (NLT)

### 5. You can have a clear conscience and rest in the heart.

Proverbs 3:21–26 My child, don't lose sight of common sense and discernment. Hang on to them, for they will refresh your soul. They are like jewels on a necklace. They keep you safe on your way, and your feet will not stumble. You can go to bed without fear; you will lie down and sleep soundly. You need not be afraid of sudden disaster or the destruction that comes upon the wicked, for the LORD is your security. He will keep your foot from being caught in a trap. (NLT)

6. Christ will give you a clear conscience.

   **Hebrews 9:14** How much more, then, will the blood of Christ, who through the eternal Spirit offered himself unblemished to God, cleanse our consciences from acts that lead to death, so that we may serve the living God! (NIV)

7. A guilty conscience can be cleansed.

   **Hebrews 10:22** Let us draw near to God with a sincere heart and with the full assurance that faith brings, having our hearts sprinkled to cleanse us from a guilty conscience and having our bodies washed with pure water. (NIV)

# Contentment, Coveting, Priorities

Note: To be content is to accept in faith, with a thankful heart and submissive spirit, that which God in his grace and wisdom ordains for us.

1. **Godliness with contentment is great gain.**

   **1 Timothy 6:6** But godliness actually is a means of great gain when accompanied by contentment. (NASB)

2. **Learn contentment, for love of money brings misery.**

   **1 Timothy 6:7–10** For we have brought nothing into the world, so we cannot take anything out of it either. If we have food and covering, with these we shall be content. But those who want to get rich fall into temptation and a snare and many foolish and harmful desires which plunge men into ruin and destruction. For the love of money is a root of all sorts of evil, and some by longing for it have wandered away from the faith and pierced themselves with many griefs. (NASB)

3. **Keep free from the love of money and be content.**

   **Hebrews 13:5** Keep your lives free from the love of money and be content with what you have, because God has said, "Never will I leave you; never will I forsake you" [Deut. 31:6]. (NIV)

4. **Paul learned contentment even in the most difficult circumstances of life.**

   **Philippians 4:11–13** Not that I am speaking of being in need, for I have learned in whatever situation I am to be content. I know how to be brought low, and I know how to abound. In any and every circumstance, I have learned the secret of facing plenty and hunger, abundance and need. I can do all things through him who strengthens me.

5. **Contentment promotes peace.**

   **Proverbs 17:1** Better is a dry morsel with quiet than a house full of feasting with strife.

6. **Life does not consist of what one possesses.**

   **Luke 12:15** Then He [Jesus] said to them, "Beware, and be on your guard against every form of greed; for not even when one has an abundance does his life consist of his possessions." (NASB)

7. **The parable of the rich fool teaches that life is more than material riches.**

   **Luke 12:16–21** *(The rich fool stored up things for himself but was not rich toward God, so his life was demanded of him.)*

8. **Do not allow the deceitfulness of wealth to crowd out the Word.**

   **Mark 4:1–20** *(the parable of the sower)*
   **Mark 4:7, 18–19** Other seed fell among thorns, which grew up and choked the plants, so that they did not bear grain. . . . [Other people], like seed sown among thorns, hear the word; but the worries of this life, the deceitfulness of wealth and the desires for other things come in and choke the word, making it unfruitful. (NIV)

9. **Put covetousness to death.**

   **Colossians 3:5** Put to death therefore what is earthly in you: sexual immorality, impurity, passion, evil desire, and covetousness, which is idolatry.

10. **Do not lay up earthly treasures, but heavenly treasures.**

    **Matthew 6:19–21** Do not lay up for yourselves treasures on earth, where moth and rust destroy and where thieves break in and steal, but lay up for yourselves treasures in heaven, where neither moth nor rust destroys and where thieves do not break in and steal. For where your treasure is, there your heart will be also.

**11. You can't serve two masters at one time.**

Matthew 6:24 No one can serve two masters, for either he will hate the one and love the other, or he will be devoted to the one and despise the other. You cannot serve God and money.

**12. Seek first God's kingdom.**

Matthew 6:33 But seek first the kingdom of God and his righteousness, and all these things will be added to you.

**13. Don't seek status, as the disciples did.**

Luke 9:46–48 Then his disciples began arguing about which of them was the greatest. But Jesus knew their thoughts, so he brought a little child to his side. Then he said to them, "Anyone who welcomes a little child like this on my behalf welcomes me, and anyone who welcomes me also welcomes my Father who sent me. Whoever is the least among you is the greatest." (NLT)

**14. It's better to have a simple lifestyle than to have wealth with a lot of conflict in the home.**

Proverbs 15:16–17 Better is a little with the fear of the LORD, than great treasure with trouble. Better is a dinner of herbs where love is, than a fatted calf with hatred. (NKJV)
Proverbs 17:1 Better is a dry morsel with quietness, than a house full of feasting with strife. (NKJV)

**15. Don't wear yourself out to get rich.**

Proverbs 23:4–5 Do not toil to acquire wealth; be discerning enough to desist. When your eyes light on it, it is gone, for suddenly it sprouts wings, flying like an eagle toward heaven.
Proverbs 28:6 Better is a poor man who walks in his integrity than a rich man who is crooked in his ways.

Ecclesiastes 4:6 Better is a handful of quietness than two hands full of toil and a striving after wind.

16. **Seek neither poverty nor riches.**

Proverbs 30:8–9 Remove far from me falsehood and lying; give me neither poverty nor riches; feed me with the food that is needful for me, lest I be full and deny you and say, "Who is the Lord?" or lest I be poor and steal and profane the name of my God.

17. **It's better to have wisdom than to have wealth.**

Proverbs 16:16–17 How much better to get wisdom than gold, to get insight rather than silver! The highway of the upright avoids evil; those who guard their ways preserve their lives. (NIV)

18. **A good name is more desirable than great riches.**

Proverbs 22:1 A good name is more desirable than great riches; to be esteemed is better than silver or gold. (NIV)

19. **King Ahab's unchecked covetousness finally drove him to murder.**

1 Kings 21:1–14

1 Kings 21:2–4 So Ahab spoke to Naboth, saying, "Give me your vineyard, that I may have it for a vegetable garden, because it is near, next to my house; and for it I will give you a vineyard better than it. Or, if it seems good to you, I will give you its worth in money." But Naboth said to Ahab, "The Lord forbid that I should give the inheritance of my fathers to you!" So Ahab went into his house sullen and displeased because of the word which Naboth the Jezreelite had spoken to him; for he had said, "I will not give you the inheritance of my fathers." And he lay down on his bed, and turned away his face, and would eat no food. (NKJV)

20. **King Hezekiah had his priorities turned around. In pride he displayed earthly riches, and was judged for it.**

2 Kings 20:12–19

2 Kings 20:14–19 Then Isaiah the prophet went to King Hezekiah, and said to him, "What did these men say, and from where did they come to you?" So Hezekiah said, "They came from a far country, from Babylon." And he said, "What have they seen in your house?" So Hezekiah answered, "They have seen all that is in my house; there is nothing among my treasures that I have not shown them." Then Isaiah said to Hezekiah, "Hear the word of the LORD: 'Behold, the days are coming when all that is in your house, and what your fathers have accumulated until this day, shall be carried to Babylon; nothing shall be left,' says the LORD. 'And they shall take away some of your sons who will descend from you, whom you will beget; and they shall be eunuchs in the palace of the king of Babylon.'" So Hezekiah said to Isaiah, "The word of the LORD which you have spoken is good!" For he said, "Will there not be peace and truth at least in my days?" (NKJV)

21. Habakkuk was content with God's way and trusted him even when things looked very hard.

Habakkuk 3:17–19 Though the fig tree may not blossom, nor fruit be on the vines; though the labor of the olive may fail, and the fields yield no food; though the flock may be cut off from the fold, and there be no herd in the stalls—yet I will rejoice in the LORD, I will joy in the God of my salvation. The LORD God is my strength; he will make my feet like deer's feet, and he will make me walk on my high hills. (NKJV)

22. God chastised Gehazi severely for his covetousness.

2 Kings 5:19–27 (Gehazi deceitfully obtains a gift from Naaman.)
2 Kings 5:19–20 He said to him, "Go in peace." But when Naaman had gone from him a short distance, Gehazi, the servant of Elisha the man of God, said, "See, my master has spared this Naaman the Syrian, in not accepting from his hand what he brought. As the LORD lives, I will run after him and get something from him."

2 Kings 5:27 "Therefore the leprosy of Naaman shall cling to you and to your descendants forever." So he went out from his presence a leper, like snow.

23. **Riches are meaningless; wealth is fleeting.**

Ecclesiastes 5:8–17
Ecclesiastes 5:10–11 Those who love money will never have enough. How meaningless to think that wealth brings true happiness! The more you have, the more people come to help you spend it. So what good is wealth—except perhaps to watch it slip through your fingers! (NLT)
Ecclesiastes 5:15–17 We all come to the end of our lives as naked and empty-handed as on the day we were born. We can't take our riches with us. And this, too, is a very serious problem. People leave this world no better off than when they came. All their hard work is for nothing—like working for the wind. Throughout their lives, they live under a cloud—frustrated, discouraged, and angry. (NLT)

24. **The primary goal in life must be to fear God and keep his commandments.**

Ecclesiastes 12:13–14 The end of the matter; all has been heard. Fear God and keep his commandments, for this is the whole duty of man. For God will bring every deed into judgment, with every secret thing, whether good or evil.
Matthew 6:33 But seek first the kingdom of God and his righteousness, and all these things will be added to you.

25. **What is seen is temporary, but what is unseen is eternal.**

2 Corinthians 4:18 So we don't look at the troubles we can see now; rather, we fix our gaze on things that cannot be seen. For the things we see now will soon be gone, but the things we cannot see will last forever. (NLT)

26. **Set your affections on the things above, not on things on the earth.**

Colossians 3:1–3 Since you have been raised to new life with Christ, set your sights on the realities of heaven, where Christ sits in the place of honor at God's right hand. Think about the things of heaven, not the things of earth. For you died to this life, and your real life is hidden with Christ in God. (NLT)

27. **The righteous will be ready to give liberally, rather than to be covetous.**

     **Proverbs 21:26** All day long he [the sluggard] craves and craves, but the righteous gives and does not hold back.

# Death, Eternal Life

*In the* case of the death of a child, see also Children

1. **You can face death without fear.**

   **Psalm 23:4** Yea, though I walk through the valley of the shadow of death, I will fear no evil; for You are with me; Your rod and Your staff, they comfort me. (NKJV)

2. **The believer will dwell in God's house forever.**

   **Psalm 23:6** Surely goodness and mercy shall follow me all the days of my life; and I will dwell in the house of the LORD forever. (NKJV)

   **John 14:1–4** Let not your hearts be troubled. Believe in God; believe also in me. In my Father's house are many rooms. If it were not so, would I have told you that I go to prepare a place for you? And if I go and prepare a place for you, I will come again and will take you to myself, that where I am you may be also. And you know the way to where I am going.

3. **To live is Christ; to die is gain.**

   **Philippians 1:21** For to me, to live is Christ and to die is gain. (NIV)

4. **Paul wanted both to remain here and to go home to be with the Lord, which is far better.**

   **Philippians 1:22–26**
   **Philippians 1:23–24** I am hard pressed between the two. My desire is to depart and be with Christ, for that is far better. But to remain in the flesh is more necessary on your account.

5. **The death of the Lord's saints is precious.**

   **Psalm 116:15** Precious in the sight of the LORD is the death of his faithful servants. (NIV)

6. **Those who die in the Lord are blessed.**

   **Revelation 14:13** And I heard a voice from heaven saying, "Write this: Blessed are the dead who die in the Lord from now on." "Blessed indeed," says the Spirit, "that they may rest from their labors, for their deeds follow them!"

7. **You can have comfort concerning those who have died and are asleep in Jesus.**

   **1 Thessalonians 4:13–18**
   **1 Thessalonians 4:16–18** For the Lord himself will descend from heaven with a cry of command, with the voice of an archangel, and with the sound of the trumpet of God. And the dead in Christ will rise first. Then we who are alive, who are left, will be caught up together with them in the clouds to meet the Lord in the air, and so we will always be with the Lord. Therefore encourage one another with these words.

8. **Believers who have died are absent from the body, but at home with the Lord.**

   **2 Corinthians 5:1–8** *(our heavenly dwellings)*
   **2 Corinthians 5:6–8** So we are always of good courage. We know that while we are at home in the body we are away from the Lord, for we walk by faith, not by sight. Yes, we are of good courage, and we would rather be away from the body and at home with the Lord.

9. **In life and death we are the Lord's.**

   **Romans 14:8** For if we live, we live for the Lord, or if we die, we die for the Lord; therefore whether we live or die, we are the Lord's. (NASB)

10. Jesus comforted Mary and Martha after Lazarus died. He is the resurrection and the life.

    **John 11:17–26**
    John 11:23–26 Jesus told her, "Your brother will rise again." "Yes," Martha said, "he will rise when everyone else rises, at the last day." Jesus told her, "I am the resurrection and the life. Anyone who believes in me will live, even after dying. Everyone who lives in me and believes in me will never ever die. Do you believe this, Martha?" (NLT)

11. The perishable will put on the imperishable; death will be swallowed up in victory.

    **1 Corinthians 15:54–57** Then, when our dying bodies have been transformed into bodies that will never die, this Scripture will be fulfilled: "Death is swallowed up in victory. O death, where is your victory? O death, where is your sting?" For sin is the sting that results in death, and the law gives sin its power. But thank God! He gives us victory over sin and death through our Lord Jesus Christ. (NLT)

12. Believers are co-heirs with Christ.

    **Romans 8:16–17** The Spirit himself bears witness with our spirit that we are children of God, and if children, then heirs— heirs of God and fellow heirs with Christ, provided we suffer with him in order that we may also be glorified with him.

13. Nothing—not even death—can separate us from the love of God.

    **Romans 8:35–39**
    Romans 8:38–39 For I am sure that neither death nor life, nor angels nor rulers, nor things present nor things to come, nor powers, nor height nor depth, nor anything else in all creation, will be able to separate us from the love of God in Christ Jesus our Lord.

14. When David's infant son died, he was comforted by the knowledge that one day he would go to him.

    2 Samuel 12:18–23
    2 Samuel 12:23 Now that he is dead, why should I go on fasting? Can I bring him back again? I will go to him, but he will not return to me. (NIV)

15. Jesus, the good shepherd, laid down his life for his sheep.

    John 10:14–15 I am the good shepherd. I know my own and my own know me, just as the Father knows me and I know the Father; and I lay down my life for the sheep.

16. Jesus' sheep hear his voice and follow him, and he gives them eternal life. No one can snatch them out of his hand.

    John 10:27–30 My sheep hear my voice, and I know them, and they follow me. I give them eternal life, and they will never perish, and no one will snatch them out of my hand. My Father, who has given them to me, is greater than all, and no one is able to snatch them out of the Father's hand. I and the Father are one.

17. There will be a new heaven and a new earth in which there will be no more suffering or sorrowing.

    Revelation 21:1–4 Now I saw a new heaven and a new earth, for the first heaven and the first earth had passed away. Also there was no more sea. Then I, John, saw the holy city, New Jerusalem, coming down out of heaven from God, prepared as a bride adorned for her husband. And I heard a loud voice from heaven saying, "Behold, the tabernacle of God is with men, and He will dwell with them, and they shall be His people. God Himself will be with them and be their God. And God will wipe away every tear from their eyes; there shall be no more death, nor sorrow, nor crying. There shall be no more pain, for the former things have passed away." (NKJV)

18. Jesus died so that we may live forever with him. Encourage one another with this truth.

1 Thessalonians 5:9–11 For God has not destined us for wrath, but for obtaining salvation through our Lord Jesus Christ, who died for us, so that whether we are awake or asleep, we will live together with Him. Therefore encourage one another and build up one another, just as you also are doing. (NASB)

19. All who believe in Jesus will have eternal life.

John 3:14–15 As Moses lifted up the serpent in the wilderness, even so must the Son of Man be lifted up; so that whoever believes will in Him have eternal life. (NASB)

John 3:16 For God so loved the world, that He gave His only begotten Son, that whoever believes in Him shall not perish, but have eternal life. (NASB)

John 3:36 He who believes in the Son has eternal life; but he who does not obey the Son will not see life, but the wrath of God abides on him. (NASB)

1 John 5:11–12 This is the testimony: God has given us eternal life, and this life is in his Son. Whoever has the Son has life; whoever does not have the Son of God does not have life. (NIV)

20. When Jesus comes again, he will separate the sheep from the goats.

Matthew 25:31–46

Matthew 25:31–34 But when the Son of Man comes in His glory, and all the angels with Him, then He will sit on His glorious throne. All the nations will be gathered before Him; and He will separate them from one another, as the shepherd separates the sheep from the goats; and He will put the sheep on His right, and the goats on the left. Then the King will say to those on His right, "Come, you who are blessed of My Father, inherit the kingdom prepared for you from the foundation of the world." (NASB)

Matthew 25:41 Then He will also say to those on His left, "Depart from Me, accursed ones, into the eternal fire which has been prepared for the devil and his angels." (NASB)

Matthew 25:46 These will go away into eternal punishment, but the righteous into eternal life. (NASB)

21. **After Jesus comes again, believers will be like him.**

1 John 3:1–2 See how very much our Father loves us, for he calls us his children, and that is what we are! But the people who belong to this world don't recognize that we are God's children because they don't know him. Dear friends, we are already God's children, but he has not yet shown us what we will be like when Christ appears. But we do know that we will be like him, for we will see him as he really is. (NLT)

22. **Everyone who has this hope (certainty) will strive to live a pure life.**

1 John 3:3 And all who have this eager expectation will keep themselves pure, just as he is pure. (NLT)

23. **Christians are guaranteed an inheritance that can never be destroyed.**

1 Peter 1:3–9
1 Peter 1:3–5 Blessed be the God and Father of our Lord Jesus Christ! According to his great mercy, he has caused us to be born again to a living hope through the resurrection of Jesus Christ from the dead, to an inheritance that is imperishable, undefiled, and unfading, kept in heaven for you, who by God's power are being guarded through faith for a salvation ready to be revealed in the last time.

24. **Every Christian who has fought the good fight of faith will, like Paul, receive the crown of righteousness.**

2 Timothy 4:7–8 I have fought the good fight, I have finished the race, I have kept the faith. Henceforth there is laid up for me the crown of righteousness, which the Lord, the righteous judge, will award to me on that day, and not only to me but also to all who have loved his appearing.

25. With our spiritual father, Abraham, we can, as pilgrims, look forward to the city with foundations whose architect and builder is God.

Hebrews 11:9–10 By faith he [Abraham] made his home in the promised land like a stranger in a foreign country; he lived in tents, as did Isaac and Jacob, who were heirs with him of the same promise. For he was looking forward to the city with foundations, whose architect and builder is God. (NIV)

26. Our citizenship is in heaven. There our bodies will be like the glorious body of Jesus Christ.

Philippians 3:20–21 But our citizenship is in heaven. And we eagerly await a Savior from there, the Lord Jesus Christ, who, by the power that enables him to bring everything under his control, will transform our lowly bodies so that they will be like his glorious body. (NIV)

27. Jesus' resurrection guarantees ours.

1 Corinthians 15:12–23
1 Corinthians 15:20–23 But in fact, Christ has been raised from the dead. He is the first of a great harvest of all who have died. So you see, just as death came into the world through a man, now the resurrection from the dead has begun through another man. Just as everyone dies because we all belong to Adam, everyone who belongs to Christ will be given new life. But there is an order to this resurrection: Christ was raised as the first of the harvest; then all who belong to Christ will be raised when he comes back. (NLT)

28. Paul describes the beauty and glory of our imperishable, incorruptible resurrection bodies and declares that death will be swallowed up in victory.

1 Corinthians 15:35–57

29. Jesus gives wonderful promises to all who overcome, who conquer, who fight against sin and in their love for Christ persevere.

Revelation 2:11 The one who conquers will not be hurt by the second death.

Revelation 2:26–29 The one who conquers and who keeps my works until the end, to him I will give authority over the nations, and he will rule them with a rod of iron, as when earthen pots are broken in pieces, even as I myself have received authority from my Father. And I will give him the morning star.

Revelation 3:4–5 Yet you have still a few names in Sardis, people who have not soiled their garments, and they will walk with me in white, for they are worthy. The one who conquers will be clothed thus in white garments, and I will never blot his name out of the book of life. I will confess his name before my Father and before his angels.

Revelation 3:12 The one who conquers, I will make him a pillar in the temple of my God.

Revelation 3:21–22 The one who conquers, I will grant him to sit with me on my throne, as I also conquered and sat down with my Father on his throne. He who has an ear, let him hear what the Spirit says to the churches.

# Decision Making

1. **Joshua called the Israelites to make a decision.**

   Joshua 24:14–27
   Joshua 24:14–15 "Now fear the LORD and serve him with all faithfulness. Throw away the gods your ancestors worshiped beyond the Euphrates River and in Egypt, and serve the LORD. But if serving the LORD seems undesirable to you, then choose for yourselves this day whom you will serve, whether the gods your ancestors served beyond the Euphrates, or the gods of the Amorites, in whose land you are living. But as for me and my household, we will serve the LORD." (NIV)

2. **God's people make a covenantal commitment.**

   Joshua 24:19–27
   Joshua 24:24 And the people said to Joshua, "We will serve the LORD our God and obey him." (NIV)

3. **Elijah called God's people to stop wavering.**

   1 Kings 18:16–39
   1 Kings 18:21 And Elijah came near to all the people and said, "How long will you go limping between two different opinions? If the LORD is God, follow him; but if Baal, then follow him."

4. **Today, if you hear his voice, don't harden your hearts (a warning against unbelief and rebellion).**

   Hebrews 3:7–11 Therefore, as the Holy Spirit says, "Today, if you hear his voice, do not harden your hearts as in the rebellion, on the day of testing in the wilderness, where your fathers put me to the test and saw my works for forty years. Therefore I was provoked with that generation, and said, 'They always go astray in their heart; they have not known my ways.' As I swore in my wrath, 'They shall not enter my rest.'"

5. **Moses' decision is a good example to follow.**

**Hebrews 11:24–25** By faith Moses, when he was grown up, refused to be called the son of Pharaoh's daughter, choosing rather to be mistreated with the people of God than to enjoy the fleeting pleasures of sin.

6. **Make a full commitment.**

**Romans 12:1–2** I urge you, brothers and sisters, in view of God's mercy, to offer your bodies as a living sacrifice, holy and pleasing to God—this is your true and proper worship. Do not conform to the pattern of this world, but be transformed by the renewing of your mind. Then you will be able to test and approve what God's will is—his good, pleasing and perfect will. (NIV)

# Depression

*See also* Comfort, Prayer, Providence of God, Trust

1. **Concealing sin often leads to depression. If you confess your sins and turn from them, you will find mercy.**

    Proverbs 28:13 He who covers his sins will not prosper, but whoever confesses and forsakes them will have mercy. (NKJV)

2. **Cain's depression was due to guilt.**

    Genesis 4:6–7 "Why are you so angry?" the Lord asked Cain. "Why do you look so dejected? You will be accepted if you do what is right. But if you refuse to do what is right, then watch out! Sin is crouching at the door, eager to control you. But you must subdue it and be its master." (NLT)

3. **David was very depressed until he confessed his sin of adultery.**

    Psalm 32:3–4 When I refused to confess my sin, my body wasted away, and I groaned all day long. Day and night your hand of discipline was heavy on me. My strength evaporated like water in the summer heat. (NLT)

4. **The way out of depression caused by guilt is confession and seeking God's forgiveness.**

    Psalm 32:5 Finally, I confessed all my sins to you and stopped trying to hide my guilt. I said to myself, "I will confess my rebellion to the Lord." And you forgave me! All my guilt is gone. (NLT)

    Psalm 32:1–2, 11 [Then David could sing for joy again]. Blessed is the one whose transgressions are forgiven, whose sins are covered. Blessed is the one whose sin the Lord does not count against them and in whose spirit is no deceit. . . . Rejoice in the LORD and be glad, you righteous; sing, all you who are upright in heart! (NIV)

5. **Put your hope in God when you are downcast.**

   **Psalm 42**
   **Psalm 42:5** Why are you in despair, O my soul? And why have you become disturbed within me? Hope in God, for I shall again praise Him for the help of His presence. (NASB)

6. **Words of comfort were given to the faithful of Israel as they became depressed while in Babylon. They were called to put their faith into action in their dark hour.**

   **Isaiah 40**

7. **We may experience some tough situations, but we can avoid deep depression.**

   **2 Corinthians 4:8–9** We are hard pressed on every side, but not crushed; perplexed, but not in despair; persecuted, but not abandoned; struck down, but not destroyed. (NIV)
   **2 Corinthians 4:16–18** We do not lose heart. Though outwardly we are wasting away, yet inwardly we are being renewed day by day. For our light and momentary troubles are achieving for us an eternal glory that far outweighs them all. So we fix our eyes not on what is seen, but on what is unseen, since what is seen is temporary, but what is unseen is eternal. (NIV)

8. **Think of what Paul went through, without getting depressed, sustained by God's grace.**

   **2 Corinthians 11:23–28** I have served him far more! I have worked harder, been put in prison more often, been whipped times without number, and faced death again and again. Five different times the Jewish leaders gave me thirty-nine lashes. Three times I was beaten with rods. Once I was stoned. Three times I was shipwrecked. Once I spent a whole night and a day adrift at sea. I have traveled on many long journeys. I have faced danger from rivers and from robbers. I have faced danger from my own people, the Jews, as well as from the Gentiles. I have faced danger in the cities, in the deserts, and on the seas. And I have faced danger from men who claim to be believers but are not. I have worked hard and long, enduring many sleepless nights. I have been hungry and thirsty and have often gone without food. I have shivered in the cold, without enough clothing to keep me warm. Then, besides all this, I have the daily burden of my concern for all the churches. (NLT)

# Divorce

*See also* Marriage, Husband/Wife Relationships

1. **When God instituted marriage he made it clear that the marriage bond is to be permanent.**

    Genesis 2:24 That is why a man leaves his father and mother and is united to his wife, and they become one flesh. (NIV)

2. **God rebuked the Israelites for the sin of divorce and commanded them to be faithful to their covenant vows.**

    Malachi 2:13–16

3. **God hates divorce.**

    Malachi 2:16 "For I hate divorce," says the LORD, the God of Israel, "and him who covers his garment with wrong," says the LORD of hosts. "So take heed to your spirit, that you do not deal treacherously." (NASB)

4. **Jesus says: No divorce, except in the case of adultery.**

    Matthew 5:31–32 It was also said, "Whoever divorces his wife, let him give her a certificate of divorce." But I say to you that everyone who divorces his wife, except on the ground of sexual immorality, makes her commit adultery. And whoever marries a divorced woman commits adultery.
    Matthew 19:3–9
    Matthew 19:4–6 He answered, "Have you not read that he who created them from the beginning made them male and female, and said, 'Therefore a man shall leave his father and his mother and hold fast to his wife, and they shall become one flesh'? So

they are no longer two but one flesh. What therefore God has joined together, let not man separate."

5. **Husband and wife are bound together until death separates them.**

   Romans 7:1–3 Now, dear brothers and sisters—you who are familiar with the law—don't you know that the law applies only while a person is living? For example, when a woman marries, the law binds her to her husband as long as he is alive. But if he dies, the laws of marriage no longer apply to her. So while her husband is alive, she would be committing adultery if she married another man. But if her husband dies, she is free from that law and does not commit adultery when she remarries. (NLT)

6. **Mosaic law speaks of a bill of divorcement.**

   **Deuteronomy 24:1–4**

7. **A believer may not initiate a divorce from an unbelieving spouse.**

   **1 Corinthians 7:10–16**

8. **If the unbelieving spouse wants to depart, he or she may do so.**

   1 Corinthians 7:15 But if the unbeliever leaves, let it be so. The brother or the sister is not bound in such circumstances. (NIV)

9. **The believing spouse must seek reconciliation when trouble arises.**

   Romans 12:18 Do all that you can to live in peace with everyone. (NLT)

   Matthew 5:23–24 So if you are presenting a sacrifice at the altar in the Temple and you suddenly remember that someone has something against you, leave your sacrifice there at the altar. Go and be reconciled to that person. Then come and offer your sacrifice to God. (NLT)

   Matthew 18:15–17 If another believer sins against you, go privately and point out the offense. If the other person listens and confesses it, you have won that person back. But if you are unsuccessful, take one or two others with you and go back again, so that everything you say may be confirmed by two or three witnesses. If the person still refuses to listen, take your case to the church. Then if he or she won't accept the church's decision, treat that person as a pagan or a corrupt tax collector. (NLT)

# Example

## *(Good or Bad)*

1. **Be a godly example for others to follow.**

   **1 Timothy 4:12** Let no one look down on your youthfulness, but rather in speech, conduct, love, faith and purity, show yourself an example of those who believe. (NASB)

2. **Pastors and elders are to be good examples for the flock.**

   **1 Peter 5:2–4** Be shepherds of God's flock that is under your care, watching over them—not because you must, but because you are willing, as God wants you to be; not pursuing dishonest gain, but eager to serve; not lording it over those entrusted to you, but being examples to the flock. And when the Chief Shepherd appears, you will receive the crown of glory that will never fade away. (NIV)

3. **The apostle Paul set a godly example to teach others how a Christian ought to live.**

   **1 Corinthians 4:15–16** In Christ Jesus I became your father through the gospel. Therefore I urge you to imitate me. (NIV)

   **1 Corinthians 11:1** Follow my example, as I follow the example of Christ. (NIV)

   **2 Thessalonians 3:7–8** For you yourselves know how you ought to follow our example, because we did not act in an undisciplined manner among you, nor did we eat anyone's bread without paying for it, but with labor and hardship we kept working night and day so that we would not be a burden to any of you. (NASB)

4. Paul taught new Christians at Thessalonica by his godly example and so they soon became good examples for others.

1 Thessalonians 1:5–7 You know what kind of men we proved to be among you for your sake. You also became imitators of us and of the Lord, having received the word in much tribulation with the joy of the Holy Spirit, so that you became an example to all the believers in Macedonia and in Achaia. (NASB)

5. Jesus warns us never to set a bad example and cause others to sin.

Matthew 5:19 Whoever then annuls one of the least of these commandments, and teaches others to do the same, shall be called least in the kingdom of heaven; but whoever keeps and teaches them, he shall be called great in the kingdom of heaven. (NASB)

Matthew 18:6 But whoever causes one of these little ones who believe in me to stumble, it would be better for him to have a heavy millstone hung around his neck, and to be drowned in the depth of the sea. (NASB)

Luke 17:1–3 He said to His disciples, "It is inevitable that stumbling blocks come, but woe to him through whom they come! It would be better for him if a millstone were hung around his neck and he were thrown into the sea, than that he would cause one of these little ones to stumble. Be on your guard!" (NASB)

6. Don't ever put a stumbling block in another person's way.

Romans 14:13 Therefore let us not judge one another anymore, but rather determine this—not to put an obstacle or a stumbling block in a brother's way. (NASB)

7. One must be ready to give up that which is in itself indifferent rather than to cause another to sin.

Romans 14:1–21
Romans 14:19–21 So then we pursue the things which make for peace and the building up of one another. Do not tear down the work of God for the sake of food. All things indeed are clean, but they are evil for the man who eats and gives offense.

It is good not to eat meat or to drink wine, or to do anything by which your brother stumbles. (NASB)

**1 Corinthians 8:1–13** *(Paul deals with the matter of eating food sacrificed to idols.)*

**1 Corinthians 8:9–13** But take care that this right of yours does not somehow become a stumbling block to the weak. For if anyone sees you who have knowledge eating in an idol's temple, will he not be encouraged, if his conscience is weak, to eat food offered to idols? And so by your knowledge this weak person is destroyed, the brother for whom Christ died. Thus, sinning against your brothers and wounding their conscience when it is weak, you sin against Christ. Therefore, if food makes my brother stumble, I will never eat meat, lest I make my brother stumble.

# False Prophets, Teachers

Note: False prophets and false teachers arise from within the church. They always put on a false front and often mix truth with error. They are, therefore, often difficult to detect. This requires watchfulness.

1. **False prophets promise peace when there is no peace. They tell you that you can live in sin and God will not punish you.**

   Jeremiah 14:11–16
   Jeremiah 14:13–14 Then I said: "Ah, Lord God, behold, the prophets say to them, 'You shall not see the sword, nor shall you have famine, but I will give you assured peace in this place.'" And the LORD said to me: "The prophets are prophesying lies in my name. I did not send them, nor did I command them or speak to them. They are prophesying to you a lying vision, worthless divination, and the deceit of their own minds."

2. **God reveals the terrible damage false prophets do in the church and warns against them.**

   Jeremiah 23:1–40

3. **God warns against the false shepherds who destroy and scatter the flock.**

   Jeremiah 23:1–4 "Woe to the shepherds who destroy and scatter the sheep of My pasture!" says the LORD. Therefore thus says the LORD God of Israel against the shepherds who feed My people: "You have scattered My flock, driven them away, and not attended to them. Behold, I will attend to you for the evil of your doings," says the LORD. "But I will gather the remnant of My flock out of all countries where I have driven them, and bring them back to their folds; and they shall be fruitful and increase.

I will set up shepherds over them who will feed them; and they shall fear no more, nor be dismayed, nor shall they be lacking," says the LORD. (NKJV)

4. **God warns his people not to listen to the false prophets who say that he will not punish unrepentant sinners.**

Jeremiah 23:16–24

Jeremiah 23:16–20 Thus says the LORD of hosts: "Do not listen to the words of the prophets who prophesy to you. They make you worthless; they speak a vision of their own heart, not from the mouth of the LORD. They continually say to those who despise Me, 'The LORD has said, "you shall have peace"'; and to everyone who walks according to the dictates of his own heart, they say, 'No evil shall come upon you.'" For who has stood in the counsel of the LORD, and has perceived and heard His word? Who has marked His word and heard it? Behold, a whirlwind of the LORD has gone forth in fury —a violent whirlwind! It will fall violently on the head of the wicked. The anger of the LORD will not turn back until He has executed and performed the thoughts of His heart. In the latter days you will understand it perfectly. (NKJV)

Ezekiel 13:1–16

Ezekiel 13:10–12 Because, indeed, because they have seduced my people, saying, "Peace!" when there is no peace—and one builds a wall, and they plaster it with untempered mortar— say to those who plaster it with untempered mortar, that it will fall. There will be flooding rain, and you, O great hailstones, shall fall; and a stormy wind shall tear it down. Surely, when the wall has fallen, will it not be said to you, "Where is the mortar with which you plastered it?" (NKJV)

5. **Jesus warns against false prophets who are wolves in sheep's clothing.**

Matthew 7:15 Beware of false prophets, who come to you in sheep's clothing, but inwardly they are ravenous wolves. (NKJV)

6. Paul warns that savage wolves will come, even from within the church, and will not spare the flock.

Acts 20:29–31 I know that after my departure fierce wolves will come in among you, not sparing the flock; and from among your own selves will arise men speaking twisted things, to draw away the disciples after them. Therefore be alert, remembering that for three years I did not cease night or day to admonish everyone with tears.

7. Peter warns that false teachers will arise within the church and secretly introduce destructive heresies.

2 Peter 2:1–3 But false prophets also arose among the people, just as there will be false teachers among you, who will secretly bring in destructive heresies, even denying the Master who bought them, bringing upon themselves swift destruction. And many will follow their sensuality, and because of them the way of truth will be blasphemed. And in their greed they will exploit you with false words. Their condemnation from long ago is not idle, and their destruction is not asleep.

8. False teachers masquerade also as angels of light.

2 Corinthians 11:1–15

2 Corinthians 11:13–15 For such men are false apostles, deceitful workmen, disguising themselves as apostles of Christ. And no wonder, for even Satan disguises himself as an angel of light. So it is no surprise if his servants, also, disguise themselves as servants of righteousness. Their end will correspond to their deeds.

9. Don't be like the Galatian Christians who were easily led away from the purity of the gospel by false teachers, the Judaizers.

Galatians 3:1–9

Galatians 3:1 O foolish Galatians! Who has bewitched you? It was before your eyes that Jesus Christ was publicly portrayed as crucified.

10. Test the spirits (by the Word of God) to see whether or not they are from God.

   **1 John 4:1–3**
   **1 John 4:1** Beloved, do not believe every spirit, but test the spirits, whether they are of God; because many false prophets have gone out into the world. (NKJV)

11. Be like the Berean Christians.

   **Acts 17:11** Now the Berean Jews were of more noble character than those in Thessalonica, for they received the message with great eagerness and examined the Scriptures every day to see if what Paul said was true. (NIV)

12. Jesus commends the church that tests what it hears, and will not tolerate false teachers.

   **Revelation 2:2–3** *(To the church in Ephesus)* I know your works, your labor, your patience, and that you cannot bear those who are evil. And you have tested those who say they are apostles and are not, and have found them liars; and you have persevered and have patience, and have labored for My name's sake and have not become weary. (NKJV)

13. A horrible, shocking thing happened in Jeremiah's time. False prophets spread lies and the people loved it.

   **Jeremiah 5:30–31** An astonishing and horrible thing has been committed in the land: The prophets prophesy falsely, and the priests rule by their own power; and My people love to have it so. But what will you do in the end? (NKJV)

14. God calls his people to repent and listen to the faithful prophets.

   **Jeremiah 6**
   **Jeremiah 6:16–17** Thus says the LORD: "Stand in the ways and see, and ask for the old paths, where the good way is, and walk in it; then you will find rest for your souls. But they said, 'We will not walk in it.' Also, I set watchmen over you, saying, 'Listen to

the sound of the trumpet!' But they said, 'We will not listen.'"
(NKJV)

15. **Don't allow false teachers to entice you back into slavery to sin.**

**2 Peter 2:17–22**
**2 Peter 2:18–19** For, speaking loud boasts of folly, they entice
by sensual passions of the flesh those who are barely escaping
from those who live in error. They promise them freedom, but
they themselves are slaves of corruption. For whatever overcomes
a person, to that he is enslaved.

16. **Be on your guard so that you will not be carried away by lawless men.**

2 Peter 3:17–18 You therefore, beloved, knowing this beforehand, take care that you are not carried away with the error of
lawless people and lose your own stability. But grow in the grace
and knowledge of our Lord and Savior Jesus Christ. To him be
the glory both now and to the day of eternity. Amen.

# Fear

*See also* Comfort, Prayer, Trust

1. **Believers need not be slaves to fear.**

   **Romans 8:15** For you did not receive the spirit of slavery to fall back into fear, but you have received the Spirit of adoption as sons, by whom we cry, "Abba! Father!"

   **2 Timothy 1:7** For God gave us a spirit not of fear but of power and love and self-control.

2. **You need not be afraid if God is your helper.**

   **Hebrews 13:5–6** God has said, "Never will I leave you; never will I forsake you" [Deut. 31:6]. So we say with confidence, "The Lord is my helper; I will not be afraid. What can mere mortals do to me?" [Ps. 118:6–7]. (NIV)

3. **The Lord is the believer's light; he need not fear.**

   **Psalm 27:1** The LORD is my light and my salvation; whom shall I fear? The LORD is the strength of my life; of whom shall I be afraid? (NKJV)

4. **Trust in God casts out fear.**

   **Psalm 56:3–4** When I am afraid, I put my trust in you. In God, whose word I praise, in God I trust; I shall not be afraid. What can flesh do to me?

   **Psalm 56:10–11** In God, whose word I praise, in the LORD, whose word I praise, in God I trust; I shall not be afraid. What can man do to me?

5. Do not fear those who can kill the body.

Matthew 10:28 And do not fear those who kill the body but cannot kill the soul. But rather fear Him who is able to destroy both soul and body in hell. (NKJV)

6. Don't be afraid; God cares for sparrows, and he will surely care for you.

Matthew 10:29–30 Are not two sparrows sold for a copper coin? And not one of them falls to the ground apart from your Father's will. But the very hairs of your head are all numbered. Do not fear therefore; you are of more value than many sparrows. (NKJV)

7. Perfect love drives out fear.

1 John 4:18 There is no fear in love, but perfect love casts out fear. For fear has to do with punishment, and whoever fears has not been perfected in love.

# Forgiveness of Sins

## *(God's Forgiveness)*

*See also* **Salvation**

1. **Believers are made as white as snow.**

   Isaiah 1:18 "Come now, let us reason together," says the LORD: "though your sins are like scarlet, they shall be as white as snow; though they are red like crimson, they shall become like wool."

2. **David sang joyfully after he repented of adultery and God forgave him.**

   Psalm 32:1–2 Blessed is the one whose transgression is forgiven, whose sin is covered. Blessed is the man against whom the LORD counts no iniquity, and in whose spirit there is no deceit.

3. **David was depressed until he repented and was forgiven.**

   Psalm 32:3–4 For when I kept silent, my bones wasted away through my groaning all day long. For day and night your hand was heavy upon me; my strength was dried up as by the heat of summer.

4. **God readily forgave David when he repented and confessed his sin.**

   Psalm 32:5 I acknowledged my sin to you, and I did not cover my iniquity; I said, "I will confess my transgressions to the LORD," and you forgave the iniquity of my sin.

5. David's confession of sin and his cry for forgiveness occurred only by God's grace.

    Psalm 51:1–17

6. God will not despise a broken spirit and contrite heart.

    Psalm 51:17 The sacrifices of God are a broken spirit; a broken and contrite heart, O God, you will not despise.

7. How great is God's forgiveness!

    Psalm 103:8–12 The LORD is merciful and gracious, slow to anger, and abounding in mercy. He will not always strive with us, nor will He keep His anger forever. He has not dealt with us according to our sins, nor punished us according to our iniquities. For as the heavens are high above the earth, so great is His mercy toward those who fear Him; as far as the east is from the west, so far has He removed our transgressions from us. (NKJV)

8. The Lord is kind and forgiving.

    Psalm 86:4–7 Gladden the soul of your servant, for to you, O Lord, do I lift up my soul. For you, O Lord, are good and forgiving, abounding in steadfast love to all who call upon you. Give ear, O LORD, to my prayer; listen to my plea for grace. In the day of my trouble I call upon you, for you answer me.

9. God calls sinners to seek him and promises them forgiveness when they repent.

    Isaiah 55:6–7 Seek the LORD while he may be found; call upon him while he is near; let the wicked forsake his way, and the unrighteous man his thoughts; let him return to the LORD, that he may have compassion on him, and to our God, for he will abundantly pardon.

10. Jesus extends a loving invitation.

    Matthew 11:28–30 Come to Me, all you who labor and are heavy laden, and I will give you rest. Take My yoke upon you and learn from Me, for I am gentle and lowly in heart, and you will find rest for your souls. For My yoke is easy and My burden is light. (NKJV)

11. **Jesus forgave the penitent woman.**

Luke 7:36–50

Luke 7:47–50 "Therefore I say to you, her sins, which are many, are forgiven, for she loved much. But to whom little is forgiven, the same loves little." Then He said to her, "Your sins are forgiven." And those who sat at the table with Him began to say to themselves, "Who is this who even forgives sins?" Then He said to the woman, "Your faith has saved you. Go in peace." (NKJV)

12. **Jesus forgave the murderer on the cross (an example of one saved only by grace).**

Luke 23:43 And he said to him, "Truly, I say to you, today you will be with me in Paradise."

13. **Sinners are forgiven when they repent and believe in Jesus.**

Luke 15:11–32 *(the parable of the prodigal son)*

14. **Jesus tells us to pray for forgiveness.**

Matthew 6:12 And forgive us our debts, as we also have forgiven our debtors.

15. **We are justified (cleared of all guilt) by faith in Jesus; in him we find peace.**

Romans 3:21–25 But now the righteousness of God has been manifested apart from the law, although the Law and the Prophets bear witness to it—the righteousness of God through faith in Jesus Christ for all who believe. For there is no distinction: for all have sinned and fall short of the glory of God, and are justified by his grace as a gift, through the redemption that is in Christ Jesus, whom God put forward as a propitiation by his blood, to be received by faith. This was to show God's righteousness, because in his divine forbearance he had passed over former sins.

Romans 5:1 Therefore, since we have been justified by faith, we have peace with God through our Lord Jesus Christ.

Romans 8:1, 4 Therefore, there is now no condemnation for those who are in Christ Jesus. . . . [for those] who do not live according to the flesh but according to the Spirit. (NIV)

### 16. In love Jesus died to make us holy; we are without blemish.

Ephesians 5:25–27 Husbands, love your wives, as Christ loved the church and gave himself up for her, that he might sanctify her, having cleansed her by the washing of water with the word, so that he might present the church to himself in splendor, without spot or wrinkle or any such thing, that she might be holy and without blemish.

Hebrews 10:10 And by that will we have been sanctified through the offering of the body of Jesus Christ once for all.

Hebrews 10:14 For by a single offering he has perfected for all time those who are being sanctified.

### 17. The blood of Jesus Christ cleanses from all sin.

1 John 1:7 But if we walk in the light as He is in the light, we have fellowship with one another, and the blood of Jesus Christ His Son cleanses us from all sin. (NKJV)

### 18. God graciously forgives when we confess our sins before him.

1 John 1:9 If we confess our sins, He is faithful and just to forgive us our sins and to cleanse us from all unrighteousness. (NKJV)

Proverbs 28:13–14 He who covers his sins will not prosper, but whoever confesses and forsakes them will have mercy. Happy is the man who is always reverent, but he who hardens his heart will fall into calamity. (NKJV)

### 19. God forgives and saves all kinds of sinners, no matter how bad they are; he changes them.

1 Corinthians 6:9–11 Do you not know that the unrighteous will not inherit the kingdom of God? Do not be deceived: neither the sexually immoral, nor idolaters, nor adulterers, nor men

who practice homosexuality, nor thieves, nor the greedy, nor drunkards, nor revilers, nor swindlers will inherit the kingdom of God. And such were some of you. But you were washed, you were sanctified, you were justified in the name of the Lord Jesus Christ and by the Spirit of our God.

20. **Zechariah had a vision of the high priest in filthy clothes, which were removed and replaced with pure white garments.**

Zechariah 3:1–5 Then he showed me Joshua the high priest standing before the angel of the LORD, and Satan standing at his right hand to accuse him. And the LORD said to Satan, "The Lord rebuke you, O Satan! The LORD who has chosen Jerusalem rebuke you! Is not this a brand plucked from the fire?" Now Joshua was standing before the angel, clothed with filthy garments. And the angel said to those who were standing before him, "Remove the filthy garments from him." And to him he said, "Behold, I have taken your iniquity away from you, and I will clothe you with pure vestments." And I said, "Let them put a clean turban on his head." So they put a clean turban on his head and clothed him with garments. And the angel of the LORD was standing by.

21. **The Samaritan woman, an adulteress, was saved by Jesus; she received living water.**

John 4:4–26
John 4:13–14 And whatever you ask in My name, that I will do, that the Father may be glorified in the Son. If you ask anything in My name, I will do it. (NKJV)

22. **Peter, who denied Jesus, was forgiven and reinstated in his office.**

John 21:15–16 *(Jesus even entrusted Peter with his precious people, for whom he died on the cross.)* Jesus said, "Feed my lambs. . . . Take care of my sheep." (NIV)

23. **Jesus gave us the parable of the Pharisee and the tax collector.**

Luke 18:9–14 *(The proud, self-righteous Pharisee was not justified or forgiven. But the humbled tax collector was justified and could go home with peace in his heart.)*

Luke 18:13–14 And the tax collector, standing afar off, would not so much as raise his eyes to heaven, but beat his breast, saying, "God, be merciful to me a sinner!" I tell you, this man went down to his house justified rather than the other; for everyone who exalts himself will be humbled, and he who humbles himself will be exalted. (NKJV)

24. Troubled sinners cry out for mercy, and God graciously forgives; he restores us to his love and favor.

Psalm 130
Psalm 130:3–4 If you, O LORD, should mark iniquities, O Lord, who could stand? But with you there is forgiveness, that you may be feared.

25. Believers are rescued from the dominion of darkness. They are brought into Jesus' eternal kingdom and are forgiven of all their sins.

Colossians 1:13–14 He has delivered us from the domain of darkness and transferred us to the kingdom of his beloved Son, in whom we have redemption, the forgiveness of sins.

26. God has lavished his grace on us, choosing us, forgiving us of all our sins through the shed blood of Christ.

Ephesians 1:3–10
Ephesians 1:7–8 In him we have redemption through his blood, the forgiveness of our trespasses, according to the riches of his grace, which he lavished upon us, in all wisdom and insight.

27. The prayer for forgiveness must be accompanied by repentance.

1 Kings 8:33–36, 46–53 (Solomon, at the dedication of the temple, prayed that God would forgive his people if and when they should repent of their sin and sincerely serve him.)
1 Kings 8:33–36 If your people Israel are defeated by their enemies because they have sinned against you, and if they turn to you and acknowledge your name and pray to you here in this temple, then hear from heaven and forgive the sin of your people Israel and return them to this land you gave their ancestors. If

the skies are shut up and there is no rain because your people have sinned against you, and if they pray toward this Temple and acknowledge your name and turn from their sins because you have punished them, then hear from heaven and forgive the sins of your servants, your people Israel. Teach them to follow the right path, and send rain on your land that you have given to your people as their special possession. (NLT)

28. **Nehemiah wept and confessed the sins of God's people.**

Nehemiah 1:6–7 Let Your ear now be attentive and Your eyes open to hear the prayer of Your servant which I am praying before You now, day and night, on behalf of the sons of Israel Your servants, confessing the sins of the sons of Israel which we have sinned against You; I and my father's house have sinned. We have acted very corruptly against You and have not kept the commandments, nor the statutes, nor the ordinances which You commanded Your servant Moses. (NASB)

29. **God sweeps our sins away and wants us to sing for joy!**

Isaiah 44:22–23 I have wiped out your transgressions like a thick cloud and your sins like a heavy mist. Return to Me, for I have redeemed you. Shout for joy, O heavens, for the LORD has done it! Shout joyfully, you lower parts of the earth; break forth into a shout of joy, you mountains, O forest, and every tree in it; for the LORD has redeemed Jacob and in Israel He shows forth His glory. (NASB)

30. **David prayed that the Lord would forgive the sins of his youth.**

Psalm 25:7 Do not remember the sins of my youth or my transgressions; according to Your lovingkindness remember me, for Your goodness' sake, O LORD. (NASB)

31. **All the prophets testify that through faith in Jesus we have forgiveness of sins.**

Acts 10:43 Of Him all the prophets bear witness that through His name everyone who believes in Him receives forgiveness of sins. (NASB)

32. Jesus is the only one through whom one can be saved and enjoy the forgiveness of sins.

Acts 4:12 And there is salvation in no one else, for there is no other name under heaven given among men by which we must be saved.

1 Timothy 2:5–6 For there is one God, and there is one mediator between God and men, the man Christ Jesus, who gave himself as a ransom for all, which is the testimony given at the proper time.

33. Salvation, the forgiveness of sins, is only by grace, through faith in Jesus Christ.

Ephesians 2:8–9 For by grace you have been saved through faith. And this is not your own doing; it is the gift of God, not a result of works, so that no one may boast.

34. When people repent, and in faith seek the Lord, he graciously forgives their sins, hurls their iniquities, as it were, into the depths of the sea, and remembers them no more.

Micah 7:18–19 Who is a God like you, who pardons sin and forgives the transgression of the remnant of his inheritance? You do not stay angry forever but delight to show mercy. You will again have compassion on us; you will tread our sins underfoot and hurl all our iniquities into the depths of the sea. (NIV)

35. God reconciles us to himself through Christ and counts our sins against us no more.

2 Corinthians 5:18–19 All this is from God, who through Christ reconciled us to himself and gave us the ministry of reconciliation; that is, in Christ God was reconciling the world to himself, not counting their trespasses against them, and entrusting to us the message of reconciliation.

# Forgiving Others

### 1. We must forgive our debtors.

Matthew 6:12 And forgive us our debts, as we also have forgiven our debtors. (NASB)

### 2. Forgiving others is an absolute necessity.

Matthew 6:14–15 For if you forgive others for their transgressions, your heavenly Father will also forgive you. But if you do not forgive others, then your Father will not forgive your transgressions. (NASB)

### 3. Jesus says we must forgive often.

Matthew 18:21–22 Then Peter came and said to Him, "Lord, how often shall my brother sin against me and I forgive him? Up to seven times?" Jesus said to him, "I do not say to you, up to seven times, but up to seventy times seven." (NASB)

Luke 17:3–4 Be on your guard! If your brother sins, rebuke him; and if he repents, forgive him. And if he sins against you seven times a day, and returns to you seven times, saying, "I repent," forgive him. (NASB)

### 4. The parable of the unmerciful servant shows how sinful it is not to forgive; God sends judgment on this sin.

Matthew 18:23–25

### 5. Put away bitterness and anger; forgive as God forgives.

Ephesians 4:31–32 Let all bitterness and wrath and anger and clamor and slander be put away from you, along with all malice. Be kind to one another, tender-hearted, forgiving each other, just as God in Christ also has forgiven you. (NASB)

6. **Be imitators of God.**

   Ephesians 5:1–2 Therefore be imitators of God, as beloved children; and walk in love, just as Christ also loved you and gave Himself up for us, an offering and a sacrifice to God as a fragrant aroma. (NASB)

7. **The father of the prodigal son forgave him and accepted him as completely as if he had not sinned. This father represents God. Thus Jesus reveals how God treats repentant sinners.**

   Luke 15:20–24

8. **Jesus commands us to forgive others.**

   Mark 11:25 And when you stand praying, if you hold anything against anyone, forgive them, so that your Father in heaven may forgive you your sins. (NIV)

9. **Love keeps no record of wrongs.**

   1 Corinthians 13:5 [Love] keeps no record of wrongs. (NIV)

10. **Love covers (overlooks) a multitude of sins.**

    1 Peter 4:8 Above all, love each other deeply, because love covers over a multitude of sins. (NIV)

11. **Restore with gentleness one who has fallen into sin.**

    Galatians 6:1 Brethren, even if anyone is caught in any trespass, you who are spiritual, restore such a one in a spirit of gentleness; each one looking to yourself, so that you too will not be tempted. (NASB)

12. **Paul tells us we must forgive and restore one who has sinned against us.**

    2 Corinthians 2:5–11

13. **Forgive a repentant sinner and affirm your love.**

    **2 Corinthians 2:7–8** Now, however, it is time to forgive and comfort him. Otherwise he may be overcome by discouragement. So I urge you now to reaffirm your love for him. (NLT)

14. **When we forgive others, we outwit Satan.**

    **2 Corinthians 2:10–11** Anyone you forgive, I also forgive. And what I have forgiven—if there was anything to forgive—I have forgiven in the sight of Christ for your sake, in order that Satan might not outwit us. For we are not unaware of his schemes. (NIV)

15. **Joseph forgave his brothers for selling him into slavery and treated them kindly.**

    **Genesis 45**
    **Genesis 45:4–5** "Please, come closer," he said to them. So they came closer. And he said again, "I am Joseph, your brother, whom you sold into slavery in Egypt. But don't be upset, and don't be angry with yourselves for selling me to this place. It was God who sent me here ahead of you to preserve your lives." (NLT)

    **Genesis 45:9–11** "Now hurry back to my father and tell him, 'This is what your son Joseph says: God has made me master over all the land of Egypt. So come down to me immediately! You can live in the region of Goshen, where you can be near me with all your children and grandchildren, your flocks and herds, and everything you own. I will take care of you there, for there are still five years of famine ahead of us. Otherwise you, your household, and all your animals will starve.'" (NLT)

    **Genesis 50:15–21**
    **Genesis 50:19–21** But Joseph replied, "Don't be afraid of me. Am I God, that I can punish you? You intended to harm me, but God intended it all for good. He brought me to this position so I could save the lives of many people. No, don't be afraid. I will continue to take care of you and your children." So he reassured them by speaking kindly to them. (NLT)

# Friendships

1. **Bad company corrupts good morals.**

   **1 Corinthians 15:33** Do not be misled: "Bad company corrupts good character." (NIV)

2. **Friends affect us for better or for worse.**

   **Proverbs 13:20** Walk with the wise and become wise, for a companion of fools suffers harm. (NIV)

3. **A true friend favors us by a kind rebuke when it is needed.**

   **Proverbs 28:23** Whoever rebukes a person will in the end gain favor rather than one who has a flattering tongue. (NIV)

4. **Stay away from a foolish man.**

   **Proverbs 14:7** Stay away from a fool, for you will not find knowledge on their lips. (NIV)

5. **Don't make friends with a hot-tempered man.**

   **Proverbs 22:24** Do not associate with a man given to anger; or go with a hot-tempered man. (NASB)

6. **A true friend is one who may hurt you at times for your good.**

   **Proverbs 25:11–12** Like apples of gold in settings of silver is a word spoken in right circumstances. Like an earring of gold and an ornament of fine gold is a wise reprover to a listening ear. (NASB)
   **Proverbs 27:6.** Faithful are the wounds of a friend, but deceitful are the kisses of an enemy. (NASB)

7. **A godly friend can be of great help.**

**Proverbs 27:9** Oil and perfume make the heart glad, so a man's counsel is sweet to his friend. (NASB)

**Proverbs 27:17** Iron sharpens iron, so one man sharpens another. (NASB)

8. **Jonathan and David had an ideal friendship.**

**1 Samuel 20**

**1 Samuel 20:17** And Jonathan made David swear again by his love for him, for he loved him as he loved his own soul.

**1 Samuel 23:16–17** And Jonathan, Saul's son, rose and went to David at Horesh, and strengthened his hand in God.

9. **Friendship with the world is hatred toward God.**

**James 4:4** You adulterous people, don't you know that friendship with the world means enmity against God? Therefore, anyone who chooses to be a friend of the world becomes an enemy of God. (NIV)

**1 John 2:15–17** Do not love the world or anything in the world. If anyone loves the world, love for the Father is not in them. For everything in the world—the lust of the flesh, the lust of the eyes, and the pride of life—comes not from the Father but from the world. The world and its desires pass away, but whoever does the will of God lives forever. (NIV)

# Giving

### 1. Jesus heartily approved of the widow's small gift.

Luke 21:1–4 While Jesus was in the Temple, he watched the rich people dropping their gifts in the collection box. Then a poor widow came by and dropped in two small coins. "I tell you the truth," Jesus said, "this poor widow has given more than all the rest of them. For they have given a tiny part of their surplus, but she, poor as she is, has given everything she has." (NLT)

### 2. The Lord wants us to give generously and cheerfully.

2 Corinthians 8:1–9 *(the example of the Macedonian Christians)*
2 Corinthians 8:1–5 Now, brethren, we wish to make known to you the grace of God which has been given in the churches of Macedonia, that in a great ordeal of affliction their abundance of joy and their deep poverty overflowed in the wealth of their liberality. For I testify that according to their ability, and beyond their ability, they gave of their own accord, begging us with much urging for the favor of participation in the support of the saints, and this, not as we had expected, but they first gave themselves to the Lord and to us by the will of God. (NASB)

2 Corinthians 8:11–12 But now finish doing it also, so that just as there was the readiness to desire it, so there may be also the completion of it by your ability. For if the readiness is present, it is acceptable according to what a person has, not according to what he does not have. (NASB)

2 Corinthians 9:6–7 Now this I say, he who sows sparingly will also reap sparingly, and he who sows bountifully will also reap bountifully. Each one must do just as he has purposed in his heart, not grudgingly or under compulsion, for God loves a cheerful giver. (NASB)

3. Those who are rich must give accordingly.

1 Timothy 6:17–19 Command those who are rich in this present world not to be arrogant nor to put their hope in wealth,
which is so uncertain, but to put their hope in God, who richly
provides us with everything for our enjoyment. Command them
to do good, to be rich in good deeds, and to be generous and willing to share. In this way they will lay up treasure for themselves
as a firm foundation for the coming age, so that they may take
hold of the life that is truly life. (NIV)

4. Each Christian must give as the Lord has blessed.

1 Corinthians 16:1–2 Now about the collection for the Lord's
people: Do what I told the Galatian churches to do. On the first
day of every week, each one of you should set aside a sum of
money in keeping with your income, saving it up, so that when
I come no collections will have to be made. (NIV)

5. Do not rob God of his tithes and offerings.

Malachi 3:7–10 "From the days of your fathers you have turned
aside from My statutes and have not kept them. Return to Me,
and I will return to you," says the LORD of hosts. "But you say,
'How shall we return?' Will a man rob God? Yet you are robbing
Me! But you say, 'How have we robbed you?' In tithes and offerings. You are cursed with a curse, for you are robbing Me, the
whole nation of you! Bring the whole tithe into the storehouse,
so that there may be food in My house, and test Me now in this,"
says the LORD of hosts, "if I will not open for you the windows
of heaven and pour out for you a blessing until it overflows."
(NASB)

6. Seek first the kingdom of God.

Matthew 6:33 But seek first His kingdom and His righteousness, and all these things will be added to you. (NASB)

7. Don't give to be seen of men.

Matthew 6:1–4 Beware of practicing your righteousness before men to be noticed by them; otherwise you have no reward with your Father who is in heaven. So when you give to the poor, do not sound a trumpet before you, as the hypocrites do in the synagogues and in the streets, so that they may be honored by men. Truly I say to you, they have their reward in full. But when you give to the poor, do not let your left hand know what your right hand is doing, so that your giving will be in secret; and your Father who sees what is done in secret will reward you. (NASB)

8. God requires us to be merciful and give to the poor.

Proverbs 14:21 He who despises his neighbor sins; but he who has mercy on the poor, happy is he. (NKJV)

Proverbs 19:17 He who has pity on the poor lends to the LORD, and He will pay back what he has given. (NKJV)

Proverbs 22:9 He who has a generous eye will be blessed, for he gives of his bread to the poor. (NKJV)

Matthew 5:7 Blessed are the merciful, for they shall obtain mercy. (NKJV)

Galatians 6:9–10 Let us not lose heart in doing good, for in due time we will reap if we do not grow weary. So then, while we have opportunity, let us do good to all people, and especially to those who are of the household of the faith. (NASB)

9. To give to God's children is to give to Christ.

Matthew 25:34–46

Matthew 25:34–35, 40 Then the King will say to those on his right, ". . . I was hungry and you gave me something to eat, I was thirsty and you gave me something to drink, I was a stranger and you invited me in. . . ." The King will reply, 'Truly I tell you, whatever you did for one of the least of these brothers and sisters of mine, you did for me." (NIV)

10. Be merciful and do good even to your enemies. Follow God's example.

Luke 6:27–36

Luke 6:27–28 But I say to you who hear, love your enemies, do good to those who hate you, bless those who curse you, pray for those who mistreat you. (NASB)

11. **Mere talk is not enough.**

1 John 3:16–18 We know what real love is because Jesus gave up his life for us. So we also ought to give up our lives for our brothers and sisters. If someone has enough money to live well and sees a brother or sister in need but shows no compassion—how can God's love be in that person? Dear children, let's not merely say that we love each other; let us show the truth by our actions. (NLT)

12. **We see a good example in giving as King David, the leaders of Israel, and others gave willingly and liberally for the building of the house of God.**

1 Chronicles 29:1–9

1 Chronicles 29:3 *(David sets an example.)* And now, because of my devotion to the Temple of my God, I am giving all of my own private treasures of gold and silver to help in the construction. This is in addition to the building materials I have already collected for his holy Temple. (NLT)

1 Chronicles 29:6 Then the family leaders, the leaders of the tribes of Israel, the generals and captains of the army, and the king's administrative officers all gave willingly. (NLT)

1 Chronicles 29:9 The people rejoiced over the offerings, for they had given freely and wholeheartedly to the LORD, and King David was filled with joy. (NLT)

13. **A generous giver will be blessed, but one who fails to give will suffer for it.**

Proverbs 11:24–25 One person gives freely, yet gains even more; another withholds unduly, but comes to poverty. A generous person will prosper; whoever refreshes others will be refreshed. (NIV)

14. **It is more blessed to give than to receive.**

Acts 20:35 In everything I [Paul] did, I showed you [the elders at Ephesus] that by this kind of hard work we must help the weak, remembering the words the Lord Jesus himself said: "It is more blessed to give than to receive." (NIV)

15. **Put first things first. Don't put off giving until you have what you want.**

**Haggai 1**
Haggai 1:2–4 Thus says the LORD of hosts, "This people says, 'The time has not come, even the time for the house of the LORD to be rebuilt.'" Then the word of the LORD came by Haggai the prophet, saying, "Is it time for you yourselves to dwell in your paneled houses while this house lies desolate?" (NASB)

# Homosexuality

*To help* homosexuals, see also Changing, Forgiveness of Sins, Peace, Overcoming Sin, Repentance, Sexual Immorality

1. **God unequivocally forbids homosexual activity.**

   **Leviticus 18:22** Do not have sexual relations with a man as one does with a woman; that is detestable. (NIV)

2. **God condemned Sodom and Gomorrah for their homosexuality. It is sin.**

   **Genesis 18:20–21** Then the LORD said, "The outcry against Sodom and Gomorrah is so great and their sin so grievous that I will go down and see if what they have done is as bad as the outcry that has reached me. If not, I will know." (NIV)

3. **Sodom and Gomorrah were destroyed on account of their unrepentant homosexuality.**

   **Genesis 19**
   **Genesis 19:4–5** But before they lay down, the men of the city, the men of Sodom, both young and old, all the people to the last man, surrounded the house. And they called to Lot, "Where are the men who came to you tonight? Bring them out to us, that we may know them."
   **Genesis 19:24–25** Then the LORD rained on Sodom and Gomorrah sulfur and fire from the LORD out of heaven. And he overthrew those cities, and all the valley, and all the inhabitants of the cities, and what grew on the ground.

4. The example of Sodom and Gomorrah is given as a warning for people of all ages. God holds homosexuals fully accountable for their sin.

2 Peter 2:4–10

2 Peter 2:6–10 If he condemned the cities of Sodom and Gomorrah by burning them to ashes, and made them an example of what is going to happen to the ungodly; and if he rescued Lot, a righteous man, who was distressed by the depraved conduct of the lawless (for that righteous man, living among them day after day, was tormented in his righteous soul by the lawless deeds he saw and heard)—if this is so, then the Lord knows how to rescue the godly from trials and to hold the unrighteous for punishment on the day of judgment. This is especially true of those who follow the corrupt desire of the flesh and despise authority. (NIV)

Jude 6–7 And the angels who did not keep their positions of authority but abandoned their proper dwelling—these he has kept in darkness, bound with everlasting chains for judgment on the great Day. In a similar way, Sodom and Gomorrah and the surrounding towns gave themselves up to sexual immorality and perversion. They serve as an example of those who suffer the punishment of eternal fire. (NIV)

5. God's wrath is revealed against all of the godlessness and wickedness of men—including homosexuality.

Romans 1:18–32

6. Paul describes homosexuality as a wicked perversion of God's gift.

Romans 1:26–27 That is why God abandoned them to their shameful desires. Even the women turned against the natural way to have sex and instead indulged in sex with each other. And the men, instead of having normal sexual relations with women, burned with lust for each other. Men did shameful things with other men, and as a result of this sin, they suffered within themselves the penalty they deserved. (NLT)

7. The wicked—including homosexuals—will not inherit the kingdom of God.

1 Corinthians 6:9–10 Or do you not know that the unrighteous will not inherit the kingdom of God? Do not be deceived; neither fornicators, nor idolaters, nor adulterers, nor effeminate, nor homosexuals, nor thieves, nor the covetous, nor drunkards, nor revilers, nor swindlers, will inherit the kingdom of God. (NASB)

8. There is hope for homosexuals—God forgives and cleanses persons of this sin.

1 Corinthians 6:11 Such [homosexual offenders] were some of you; but you were washed, but you were sanctified, but you were justified in the name of the Lord Jesus Christ and in the Spirit of our God. (NASB)

# Hope

*See also* Trust, Faith in God

### 1. God has solutions to our problems.

1 Corinthians 10:13 The temptations in your life are no different from what others experience. And God is faithful. He will not allow the temptation to be more than you can stand. When you are tempted, he will show you a way out so that you can endure. (NLT)

### 2. God's grace is sufficient for every need.

2 Corinthians 9:8 And God will generously provide all you need. Then you will always have everything you need and plenty left over to share with others. (NLT)

### 3. God is able to do more than we ask or imagine.

Ephesians 3:20 [God] . . . is able to do immeasurably more than all we ask or imagine, according to his power that is at work within us. (NIV)

### 4. God is always faithful.

Lamentations 3:32 Though he brings grief, he also shows compassion because of the greatness of his unfailing love. (NLT)

### 5. Hope is an anchor for the soul.

Hebrews 6:19–20 We have this as a sure and steadfast anchor of the soul, a hope that enters into the inner place behind the curtain, where Jesus has gone as a forerunner on our behalf, having become a high priest forever after the order of Melchizedek.

6. **Put your hope in God.**

   **Psalm 42**
   **Psalm 42:5** Why are you cast down, O my soul? And why are you disquieted within me? Hope in God, for I shall yet praise Him for the help of His countenance. (NKJV)

7. **Put your hope in a faithful and almighty God.**

   **Psalm 146:3–10**
   **Psalm 146:5–6** How blessed is he whose help is the God of Jacob, whose hope is in the LORD his God, who made heaven and earth, the sea and all that is in them; who keeps faith forever. (NASB)

8. **Hope produces endurance and perseverance.**

   **1 Thessalonians 1:3** As we pray to our God and Father about you, we think of your faithful work, your loving deeds, and the enduring hope you have because of our Lord Jesus Christ. (NLT)

9. **Believers have a living hope through the resurrection of Jesus Christ.**

   **1 Peter 1:3** Blessed be the God and Father of our Lord Jesus Christ, who according to His abundant mercy has begotten us again to a living hope through the resurrection of Jesus Christ from the dead. (NKJV)

10. **Trusting in the God of hope will bring you yet more joy, peace, and hope.**

    **Romans 15:13** Now may the God of hope fill you with all joy and peace in believing, that you may abound in hope by the power of the Holy Spirit. (NKJV)

# Humility, Pride

1. **Humility is a virtue most pleasing to God. Pride is a grievous sin in his sight.**

   **Proverbs 8:13** The fear of the LORD is hatred of evil. Pride and arrogance and the way of evil and perverted speech I hate.

   **Proverbs 16:5** Everyone who is proud in heart is an abomination to the LORD; assuredly, he will not be unpunished. (NASB)

   **Proverbs 16:18–19** Pride goes before destruction, and a haughty spirit before a fall. It is better to be of a lowly spirit with the poor than to divide the spoil with the proud.

   **Proverbs 21:4** Haughty eyes and a proud heart, the lamp of the wicked, are sin.

   **1 Peter 5:5–6** Likewise you younger people, submit yourselves to your elders. Yes, all of you be submissive to one another, and be clothed with humility, for "God resists the proud, but gives grace to the humble." Therefore humble yourselves under the mighty hand of God, that He may exalt you in due time. (NKJV)

2. **Listen carefully to what Jesus says.**

   **Luke 14:7–11**
   **Luke 14:11** For everyone who exalts himself will be humbled, and he who humbles himself will be exalted.

   **Matthew 5:3** Blessed are the poor in spirit, for theirs is the kingdom of heaven.

3. **Jesus rebuked the disciples (office bearers) for their proud attitude and called them to humility.**

   **Matthew 18:1–4** At that time the disciples came to Jesus, saying, "Who is the greatest in the kingdom of heaven?" And calling to him a child, he put him in the midst of them and said,

"Truly, I say to you, unless you turn and become like children, you will never enter the kingdom of heaven. Whoever humbles himself like this child is the greatest in the kingdom of heaven."

4. **He did so again at another time when they were revealing the same sinful pride.**

Matthew 20:20–28

Matthew 20:25–28 But Jesus called them to him and said, "You know that the rulers of the Gentiles lord it over them, and their great ones exercise authority over them. It shall not be so among you. But whoever would be great among you must be your servant, and whoever would be first among you must be your slave, even as the Son of Man came not to be served but to serve, and to give his life as a ransom for many."

5. **On the night before he was nailed to the cross, Jesus, the Lord and Master, gave his disciples a practical lesson by humbly washing their feet.**

John 13:2–17

John 13:12–15 So when He had washed their feet, and taken His garments and reclined at the table again, He said to them, "Do you know what I have done to you? You call Me Teacher and Lord; and you are right, for so I am. If I then, the Lord and the Teacher, washed your feet, you also ought to wash one another's feet. For I gave you an example that you also should do as I did to you." (NASB)

6. **Are you a Christian? Born again? If so, God alone gets the glory.**

Ephesians 1:11–14

Ephesians 1:11–12 In him we were also chosen, having been predestined according to the plan of him who works out everything in conformity with the purpose of his will, in order that we, who were the first to put our hope in Christ, might be for the praise of his glory. (NIV)

Ephesians 2:8–9 For it is by grace you have been saved, through faith—and this is not from yourselves, it is the gift of God—not by works, so that no one can boast. (NIV)

**John 1:11–13** He came to that which was his own, but his own did not receive him. Yet to all who did receive him, to those who believed in his name, he gave the right to become children of God—children born not of natural descent, nor of human decision or a husband's will, but born of God. (NIV)

**Titus 3:3–8**

**Titus 3:4–5** But when the kindness of God our Savior and His love for mankind appeared, He saved us, not on the basis of deeds which we have done in righteousness, but according to His mercy, by the washing of regeneration and renewing by the Holy Spirit. (NASB)

7. **If you have remained faithful to the Lord, it's by God's grace and power.**

   **John 10:27–30** My sheep hear My voice, and I know them, and they follow Me; and I give eternal life to them, and they will never perish; and no one will snatch them out of My hand. My Father, who has given them to Me, is greater than all; and no one is able to snatch them out of the Father's hand. I and the Father are one. (NASB)

8. **Jesus warns against seeking the praise of others by a proud display of piety.**

   **Matthew 6:1–8**

   **Matthew 6:1** Beware of practicing your righteousness before other people in order to be seen by them, for then you will have no reward from your Father who is in heaven.

9. **The Lord condemns those who become proud and boastful because of what he has done for them.**

   **1 Corinthians 4:7** For who makes you different from anyone else? What do you have that you did not receive? And if you did receive it, why do you boast as though you did not? (NIV)

10. All knowledge, wisdom, talents, and skills are God's gracious gifts entrusted to us. We must use them to serve and glorify him with deep humility.

Matthew 25:14–30 *(the parable of the talents)*

11. Possessing certain spiritual gifts which others do not have is no reason for pride. It is only by God's grace.

1 Corinthians 12:1–11

1 Corinthians 12:1, 4, 7, 11 Now about the gifts of the Spirit, brothers and sisters, I do not want you to be uninformed. . . . There are different kinds of gifts, but the same Spirit distributes them. . . . Now to each one the manifestation of the Spirit is given for the common good. . . . All these are the work of one and the same Spirit, and he distributes them to each one, just as he determines. (NIV)

12. Don't be conceited. Be humble. Consider others better than yourself.

Romans 9:16 It does not, therefore, depend on human desire or effort, but on God's mercy. (NIV)

Philippians 2:1–8

Philippians 2:3–4 Do nothing from selfish ambition or conceit, but in humility count others more significant than yourselves. Let each of you look not only to his own interests, but also to the interests of others.

13. Everything you have is God's gift to you.

James 1:16–17 Do not be deceived, my beloved brothers. Every good gift and every perfect gift is from above, coming down from the Father of lights with whom there is no variation or shadow due to change.

Romans 11:35–36 "Or who has given a gift to him [God] that he might be repaid?" For from him and through him and to him are all things. To him be glory forever. Amen.

14. **God warns his people not to become proud when he blesses them with prosperity.**

   Deuteronomy 8:6–18

   Deuteronomy 8:11–12, 14, 17–18 Take care lest you forget the LORD your God by not keeping his commandments and his rules and his statutes, which I command you today, lest, when you have eaten and are full and have built good houses and live in them . . . then your heart be lifted up, and you forget the LORD your God, who brought you out of the land of Egypt, out of the house of slavery. . . . Beware lest you say in your heart, "My power and the might of my hand have gotten me this wealth." You shall remember the LORD your God, for it is he who gives you power to get wealth.

15. **Jeremiah had to caution God's people not to become proud and boastful.**

   Jeremiah 9:23–24 Thus says the LORD: "Let not the wise man boast in his wisdom, let not the mighty man boast in his might, let not the rich man boast in his riches, but let him who boasts boast in this, that he understands and knows me, that I am the LORD who practices steadfast love, justice, and righteousness in the earth. For in these things I delight, declares the LORD."

16. **Those who are rich are warned not to become arrogant, or to put their hope in wealth.**

   1 Timothy 6:17–18 Command those who are rich in this present world not to be arrogant nor to put their hope in wealth, which is so uncertain, but to put their hope in God, who richly provides us with everything for our enjoyment. Command them to do good, to be rich in good deeds, and to be generous and willing to share. (NIV)

17. **All proud boasting about the future is evil.**

   James 4:13–16 Come now, you who say, "Today or tomorrow we will go to such and such a city, and spend a year there and engage in business and make a profit." Yet you do not know what your life will be like tomorrow. You are just a vapor that appears for a little while and then vanishes away. Instead, you ought to say, "If the Lord wills, we will live and also do this or that." But as it is, you boast in your arrogance; all such boasting is evil. (NASB)

18. Have you enjoyed success in service for the Lord? Paul reminds us that to God alone belongs the glory.

1 Corinthians 3:1–9
1 Corinthians 3:3–7 You are still worldly. For since there is jealousy and quarreling among you, are you not worldly? Are you not acting like mere humans? For when one says, "I follow Paul," and another, "I follow Apollos," are you not mere human beings? What, after all, is Apollos? And what is Paul? Only servants, through whom you came to believe—as the Lord has assigned to each his task. I planted the seed, Apollos watered it, but God has been making it grow. So neither the one who plants nor the one who waters is anything, but only God, who makes things grow. (NIV)

19. The proud, unrepentant, self-righteous person will not be forgiven by God. Only those who humbly confess their sins and seek forgiveness through the Lord Jesus Christ will be saved.

Luke 18:9–14 *(the parable of the proud, self-righteous Pharisee and the humble tax collector)*
Luke 18:14 I tell you, this man went to his house justified rather than the other; for everyone who exalts himself will be humbled, but he who humbles himself will be exalted. (NASB)

20. Like the apostle Paul, we must humbly reject any idea of being righteous because of our heritage or any work we have done, but trust only in Jesus Christ.

Philippians 3:3–11
Philippians 3:7–9 But what things were gain to me, these I have counted loss for Christ. Yet indeed I also count all things loss for the excellence of the knowledge of Christ Jesus my Lord, for whom I have suffered the loss of all things, and count them as rubbish, that I may gain Christ and be found in Him, not having

my own righteousness, which is from the law, but that which is through faith in Christ, the righteousness which is from God by faith. (NKJV)

**Galatians 6:12–15**

**Galatians 6:14** But God forbid that I should boast except in the cross of our Lord Jesus Christ, by whom the world has been crucified to me, and I to the world. (NKJV)

21. **The apostle Paul, a mature Christian, highly gifted, and successful in his calling, remained humble, setting an example for all of us to emulate.**

    **1 Timothy 1:15–17**

    **1 Timothy 1:15** It is a trustworthy statement, deserving full acceptance, that Christ Jesus came into the world to save sinners, among whom I am foremost of all. (NASB)

    **Romans 7:13–25** *(Paul humbly acknowledges his constant struggle against sin.)*

    **Philippians 3:12–14** Not that I have already obtained this or am already perfect, but I press on to make it my own, because Christ Jesus has made me his own. Brothers, I do not consider that I have made it my own. But one thing I do: forgetting what lies behind and straining forward to what lies ahead, I press on toward the goal for the prize of the upward call of God in Christ Jesus.

22. **God is ready to forgive and bless his people when they humble themselves before him in true repentance.**

    **2 Chronicles 7:13–16**

    **2 Chronicles 7:14** If my people who are called by my name humble themselves, and pray and seek my face and turn from their wicked ways, then I will hear from heaven and will forgive their sin and heal their land.

# Imitating Jesus

*See also* Loving and Serving Others

Note: An unbeliever cannot truly imitate Jesus. If one attempts to do so, it will be a sham. No one can become a Christian by imitating Jesus. Salvation is only by grace through faith in Jesus Christ. But if you are a Christian, you can and must imitate Him in the power of the Holy Spirit.

1. **Every Christian is predestined and called to become Christ-like.**

   **Romans 8:29–30** For those God foreknew he also predestined to be conformed to the image of his Son, that he might be the firstborn among many brothers and sisters. And those he predestined, he also called; those he called, he also justified; those he justified, he also glorified. (NIV)

2. **Christians are renewed in the image of God and are being transformed more and more into the likeness of Christ.**

   **2 Corinthians 3:18** And we all, who with unveiled faces contemplate the Lord's glory, are being transformed into his image with ever-increasing glory, which comes from the Lord, who is the Spirit. (NIV)

   **Colossians 3:9–10** Do not lie to each other, since you have taken off your old self with its practices and have put on the new self, which is being renewed in knowledge in the image of its Creator. (NIV)

   **Ephesians 4:22–24** You were taught, with regard to your former way of life, to put off your old self, which is being corrupted by its deceitful desires; to be made new in the attitude of your minds; and to put on the new self, created to be like God in true righteousness and holiness. (NIV)

3. **We must imitate Jesus; we must walk as he walked.**

1 John 2:6 Whoever says he abides in him ought to walk in the same way in which he walked.

4. **Jesus calls us to become more like he is by imitating him.**

John 13:2–11 (*Jesus purposely modeled for his disciples as he washed their feet.*)

John 13:12–15 When he had washed their feet and put on his outer garments and resumed his place, he said to them, "Do you understand what I have done to you? You call me Teacher and Lord, and you are right, for so I am. If I then, your Lord and Teacher, have washed your feet, you also ought to wash one another's feet. For I have given you an example, that you also should do just as I have done to you."

5. **Paul instructs us to imitate Jesus in order to be a blessing to others.**

Romans 15:1–3 We who are strong must be considerate of those who are sensitive about things like this. We must not just please ourselves. We should help others do what is right and build them up in the Lord. For even Christ didn't live to please himself. As the Scriptures say, "The insults of those who insult you, O God, have fallen on me." (NLT)

Ephesians 5:1–2 Imitate God, therefore, in everything you do, because you are his dear children. Live a life filled with love, following the example of Christ. He loved us and offered himself as a sacrifice for us, a pleasing aroma to God. (NLT)

6. **When someone wrongs us, we must imitate Jesus and not retaliate or get revenge in any way. He set an example for us to follow.**

1 Peter 2:18–23

1 Peter 2:20–21 For what credit is it if, when you sin and are beaten for it, you endure? But if when you do good and suffer for it you endure, this is a gracious thing in the sight of God. For to this you have been called, because Christ also suffered for you, leaving you an example, so that you might follow in his steps.

7. **Paul imitated Jesus so that he could be a good example for other Christians.**

    **1 Corinthians 11:1** Follow my example, as I follow the example of Christ. (NIV)

8. **Thessalonian Christians soon became good models for others, partly by imitating Jesus and his disciples.**

    **1 Thessalonians 1:6–7** You also became imitators of us and of the Lord, having received the word in much tribulation with the joy of the Holy Spirit, so that you became an example to all the believers in Macedonia and in Achaia. (NASB)

9. **Christ-like obedience is the way to a Christ-like enjoyment of divine love, and the way to have your joy made complete.**

    **John 15:9–11** Just as the Father has loved Me, I have also loved you; abide in My love. If you keep My commandments, you will abide in My love; just as I have kept My Father's commandments and abide in His love. These things I have spoken to you so that My joy may be in you, and that your joy may be made full. (NASB)

10. **The hope (certainty) of one day seeing Jesus face-to-face and being perfectly conformed to his image should motivate us to seek to be pure, even as he is pure.**

    **1 John 3:2–3** Dear friends, now we are children of God, and what we will be has not yet been made known. But we know that when Christ appears, we shall be like him, for we shall see him as he is. All who have this hope in him purify themselves, just as he is pure. (NIV)

11. **The risen Savior lives to God. We who have died and risen with Christ must do the same.**

    **Romans 6:10–14**
    **Romans 6:10–12** The death he died, he died to sin once for all; but the life he lives, he lives to God. In the same way, count yourselves dead to sin but alive to God in Christ Jesus. Therefore do not let sin reign in your mortal body so that you obey its evil desires. (NIV)

# Loving and Serving Others

*See also* Church, Communion of Saints; Imitating Jesus; Loving God

### 1. Love one another in response to God's love for us.

**1 John 4:9–21**

**1 John 4:9–11** By this the love of God was manifested in us, that God has sent His only begotten Son into the world so that we might live through Him. In this is love, not that we loved God, but that He loved us and sent His Son to be the propitiation for our sins. Beloved, if God so loved us, we also ought to love one another. (NASB)

**1 John 4:21** And this commandment we have from Him, that the one who loves God should love his brother also. (NASB)

### 2. Love one another deeply.

**1 Peter 1:22** Since you have in obedience to the truth purified your souls for a sincere love of the brethren, fervently love one another from the heart. (NASB)

**1 Peter 4:8** Above all, keep fervent in your love for one another, because love covers a multitude of sins. (NASB)

### 3. Genuine love is serving others.

**1 Peter 4:9–10** Offer hospitality to one another without grumbling. Each of you should use whatever gift you have received to serve others, as faithful stewards of God's grace in its various forms. (NIV)

### 4. Love is absolutely essential; one is nothing without it.

**1 Corinthians 13:1–3**

5. **Paul describes what love really is.**

**1 Corinthians 13:4–7** Love is patient, love is kind. It does not envy, it does not boast, it is not proud. It does not dishonor others, it is not self-seeking, it is not easily angered, it keeps no record of wrongs. Love does not delight in evil but rejoices with the truth. It always protects, always trusts, always hopes, always perseveres. (NIV)

6. **To love is to be devoted to one another.**

**Romans 12:9–10** Love must be sincere. Hate what is evil; cling to what is good. Be devoted to one another in love. Honor one another above yourselves. (NIV)

7. **By washing the disciples' feet, Jesus modeled for us, showing us how we must love one another.**

**John 13:2–17**
**John 13:14–15** If I then, your Lord and Teacher, have washed your feet, you also ought to wash one another's feet. For I have given you an example, that you should do as I have done to you. (NKJV)

8. **Jesus commands us to love others in the manner in which he loved us, to imitate him.**

**Matthew 16:24** Then Jesus said to His disciples, "If anyone desires to come after Me, let him deny himself, and take up his cross, and follow Me." (NKJV)
**John 13:34** A new commandment I give to you, that you love one another; as I have loved you, that you also love one another. (NKJV)
**John 15:12** This is My commandment, that you love one another as I have loved you. (NKJV)

9. **Don't be self-centered, but look out for others; in this imitate Jesus.**

**Philippians 2:3–5** Do nothing from selfishness or empty conceit, but with humility of mind regard one another as more important than yourselves; do not merely look out for your own personal interests, but also for the interests of others. Have this attitude in yourselves which was also in Christ Jesus. (NASB)

10. Jesus gave his all for us.

    Philippians 2:6–8

11. Do not seek honor and prestige but, like Jesus, be ready to serve others.

    Matthew 20:20–28
    Matthew 20:26–28 Whoever wishes to become great among you shall be your servant, and whoever wishes to be first among you shall be your slave; just as the Son of Man did not come to be served, but to serve, and to give His life a ransom for many. (NASB)

12. Attending to the needs of others is doing it for Christ.

    Matthew 25:34–40
    Matthew 25:35–36 For I was hungry, and you fed me. I was thirsty, and you gave me a drink. I was a stranger, and you invited me into your home. I was naked, and you gave me clothing. I was sick, and you cared for me. I was in prison, and you visited me. (NLT)
    Matthew 25:40 And the King will say, "I tell you the truth, when you did it to one of the least of these my brothers and sisters, you were doing it to me!" (NLT)

13. Don't become weary in doing good.

    Galatians 6:9 Let us not become weary in doing good, for at the proper time we will reap a harvest if we do not give up. (NIV)

14. Do good to all, especially to members of God's family.

    Galatians 6:10 As we have opportunity, let us do good to all people, especially to those who belong to the family of believers. (NIV)

**15. Follow the golden rule.**

Matthew 7:12 Do to others whatever you would like them to do to you. This is the essence of all that is taught in the law and the prophets. (NLT)

**16. Don't be self-centered, but please others.**

Romans 15:1–2 We who are strong have an obligation to bear with the failings of the weak, and not to please ourselves. Let each of us please his neighbor for his good, to build him up.

**17. Imitate Jesus.**

Romans 15:3 For Christ did not please himself, but as it is written, The reproaches of those who reproached you fell on me.

**18. Devote yourself to doing good.**

Titus 3:14 Our people must learn to devote themselves to doing what is good, in order to provide for urgent needs and not live unproductive lives. (NIV)

**19. You can find your life by doing good.**

Matthew 10:39 Whoever finds his life will lose it, and whoever loses his life for my sake will find it.

**20. Love your enemies and those who persecute you.**

Matthew 5:43–48 You have heard that it was said, "Love your neighbor and hate your enemy." But I tell you, love your enemies and pray for those who persecute you, that you may be children of your Father in heaven. He causes his sun to rise on the evil and the good, and sends rain on the righteous and the unrighteous. If you love those who love you, what reward will you get? Are not even the tax collectors doing that? And if you greet only your own people, what are you doing more than others? Do not even pagans do that? Be perfect, therefore, as your heavenly Father is perfect. (NIV)

Romans 12:20–21 "If your enemy is hungry, feed him; if he is thirsty, give him something to drink. In doing this, you will heap burning coals on his head." Do not be overcome by evil, but overcome evil with good. (NIV)

21. **As members of Christ's body, we all need one another; each member must use his or her gifts to serve others.**

    **1 Corinthians 12:1–31**

    **1 Corinthians 12:4–7** Now there are varieties of gifts, but the same Spirit; and there are varieties of service, but the same Lord; and there are varieties of activities, but it is the same God who empowers them all in everyone. To each is given the manifestation of the Spirit for the common good.

    **1 Peter 4:10–11** As each has received a gift, use it to serve one another, as good stewards of God's varied grace: whoever speaks, as one who speaks oracles of God; whoever serves, as one who serves by the strength that God supplies—in order that in everything God may be glorified through Jesus Christ. To him belong glory and dominion forever and ever. Amen.

22. **True freedom is to serve one another in love.**

    **Galatians 5:13–15** For you were called to freedom, brothers. Only do not use your freedom as an opportunity for the flesh, but through love serve one another. For the whole law is fulfilled in one word: "You shall love your neighbor as yourself." But if you bite and devour one another, watch out that you are not consumed by one another.

    **1 Thessalonians 4:9–11** Now concerning brotherly love you have no need for anyone to write to you, for you yourselves have been taught by God to love one another, for that indeed is what you are doing to all the brothers throughout Macedonia. But we urge you, brothers, to do this more and more, and to aspire to live quietly, and to mind your own affairs, and to work with your hands, as we instructed you, so that you may live properly before outsiders and be dependent on no one.

23. **Be a good Samaritan. Help needy persons whom the Lord puts in your pathway.**

    **Luke 10:25–37** *(the parable of the Good Samaritan)*

127

**Luke 10:36–37** "Which of these three do you think was a neighbor to the man who fell into the hands of robbers?" The expert replied, "The one who had mercy on him." Jesus told him, "Go and do likewise." (NIV)

## 24. Mere talk and good intentions avail nothing. Act! Do good!

**1 John 3:16–18** We know what real love is because Jesus gave up his life for us. So we also ought to give up our lives for our brothers and sisters. If someone has enough money to live well and sees a brother or sister in need but shows no compassion— how can God's love be in that person? Dear children, let's not merely say that we love each other; let us show the truth by our actions. (NLT)

**James 2:15–17** Suppose you see a brother or sister who has no food or clothing, and you say, "Good-bye and have a good day; stay warm and eat well"—but then you don't give that person any food or clothing. What good does that do? So you see, faith by itself isn't enough. Unless it produces good deeds, it is dead and useless. (NLT)

## 25. You know the good you ought to do. Do it, lest you sin.

**James 4:17** If anyone, then, knows the good they ought to do and doesn't do it, it is sin for them. (NIV)

# Loving God

*See also* Obedience, Loving and Serving Others, Overcoming Sin, Progressive Sanctification

1. **The believer responds to God's love and favor.**

   **Deuteronomy 6:4–7** Hear, O Israel: The LORD our God, the LORD is one. You shall love the LORD your God with all your heart and with all your soul and with all your might. And these words that I command you today shall be on your heart. You shall teach them diligently to your children, and shall talk of them when you sit in your house, and when you walk by the way, and when you lie down, and when you rise.

2. **Jesus calls us to love God above all else. He summarizes the Law as a matter of love.**

   **Matthew 22:37–40** Jesus said to him, "'You shall love the LORD your God with all your heart, with all your soul, and with all your mind.' This is the first and great commandment. And the second is like it: 'You shall love your neighbor as yourself.' On these two commandments hang all the Law and the Prophets." (NKJV)

3. **Christ's love for us must compel us to love and serve him.**

   **2 Corinthians 5:14–15** For the love of Christ controls us, having concluded this, that one died for all, therefore all died; and He died for all, so that they who live might no longer live for themselves, but for Him who died and rose again on their behalf. (NASB)

4. **Hold fast to the Lord and out of love keep his commandments.**

   **Joshua 22:5** Only be very careful to observe the commandment and the law which Moses the servant of the LORD commanded you, to love the LORD your God and walk in all His ways and keep His commandments and hold fast to Him and serve Him with all your heart and with all your soul. (NASB)

5. **To love Jesus is to obey his teaching.**

**John 14:23–24** Jesus answered and said to him, "If anyone loves Me, he will keep My word; and My Father will love him, and We will come to him and make Our abode with him. He who does not love Me does not keep My words; and the word which you hear is not Mine, but the Father's who sent Me." (NASB)

6. **Solomon tells us to respond to God's favor by serving him from the heart.**

**1 Kings 8:56–61**
**1 Kings 8:61** And may your hearts be fully committed to the LORD our God, to live by his decrees and obey his commands, as at this time. (NIV)

7. **David's charge to his son Solomon, to serve God with wholehearted devotion, is good for all of us.**

**1 Chronicles 28:9** You, my son Solomon, acknowledge the God of your father, and serve him with wholehearted devotion and with a willing mind, for the LORD searches every heart and understands every desire and every thought. If you seek him, he will be found by you; but if you forsake him, he will reject you forever. (NIV)

8. **Motivated by love, reject partying and all sinful pleasures. Instead, put on Christ.**

**Romans 13:13–14** Let us walk properly as in the daytime, not in orgies and drunkenness, not in sexual immorality and sensuality, not in quarreling and jealousy. But put on the Lord Jesus Christ, and make no provision for the flesh, to gratify its desires.

9. **God's love for us should move us to strive for purity.**

**2 Corinthians 7:1** Since we have these promises, beloved, let us cleanse ourselves from every defilement of body and spirit, bringing holiness to completion in the fear of God.

# Lust, Evil Desires

**1. Eve's sin began with lusting.**

**Genesis 3:6** So when the woman saw that the tree was good for food, and that it was a delight to the eyes, and that the tree was to be desired to make one wise, she took of its fruit and ate, and she also gave some to her husband who was with her, and he ate.

**2. Don't covet.**

**Exodus 20:17** You shall not covet your neighbor's house. You shall not covet your neighbor's wife, or his male or female servant, his ox or donkey, or anything that belongs to your neighbor. (NIV)

**3. Don't think about how to gratify the sinful nature.**

**Romans 13:14** Clothe yourselves with the Lord Jesus Christ, and do not think about how to gratify the desires of the flesh. (NIV)

**4. Say no to ungodly passions.**

**Titus 2:11–12** For the grace of God has appeared, bringing salvation for all people, training us to renounce ungodliness and worldly passions, and to live self-controlled, upright, and godly lives in the present age.

**5. Those who fulfill evil desires are objects of God's wrath.**

**Ephesians 2:3** All of us used to live that way, following the passionate desires and inclinations of our sinful nature. By our very nature we were subject to God's anger, just like everyone else. (NLT)

6. **Christ came to save us from lust and evil desires.**

    **Ephesians 2:4–5** But God is so rich in mercy, and he loved us so much, that even though we were dead because of our sins, he gave us life when he raised Christ from the dead. (It is only by God's grace that you have been saved!) (NLT)

7. **Don't conform to evil desires, but be holy.**

    **1 Peter 1:14–16** As obedient children, do not be conformed to the passions of your former ignorance, but as he who called you is holy, you also be holy in all your conduct, since it is written, "You shall be holy, for I am holy."

8. **Live by the Spirit to overcome the lusts of the flesh.**

    **Galatians 5:16** But I say, walk by the Spirit, and you will not gratify the desires of the flesh.

9. **Those who live according to the sinful nature have their minds set on what that nature desires.**

    **Romans 8:5–8** For those who live according to the flesh set their minds on the things of the flesh, but those who live according to the Spirit set their minds on the things of the Spirit. To set the mind on the flesh is death, but to set the mind on the Spirit is life and peace. For the mind that is set on the flesh is hostile to God, for it does not submit to God's law; indeed, it cannot. Those who are in the flesh cannot please God.

# Marriage, Husband/Wife Relationships

*See also* Peacemakers, Peacekeepers

1. **Marriage was instituted and designed by God.**

   **Genesis 2:18–25**

2. **At the heart of marriage is companionship and intimacy, which both husband and wife must promote.**

   **Genesis 2:18, 24** The Lord God said, "It is not good for the man to be alone. I will make a helper suitable for him." . . . That is why a man leaves his father and mother and is united to his wife, and they become one flesh. (NIV)

3. **The relationship between husband and wife is similar to that between Christ and the church.**

   **Ephesians 5:23** For a husband is the head of his wife as Christ is the head of the church. He is the Savior of his body, the church. (NLT)

   **Ephesians 5:31–32** As the Scriptures say, "A man leaves his father and mother and is joined to his wife, and the two are united into one." This is a great mystery, but it is an illustration of the way Christ and the church are one. (NLT)

4. **The husband is the head of the wife and the home.**

   **Ephesians 5:23** For a husband is the head of his wife as Christ is the head of the church. He is the Savior of his body, the church. (NLT)

5. **Husbands must love their wives as Christ loved the church.**

   **Ephesians 5:25** For husbands, this means love your wives, just as Christ loved the church. He gave up his life for her. (NLT)

6. **Husbands must exercise headship in love.**

   **Ephesians 5:25–33**
   **Colossians 3:19** Husbands, love your wives and never treat them harshly. (NLT)

7. **Husbands must treat their wives with respect and as equal heirs of God's gifts.**

   **1 Peter 3:7** You husbands in the same way, live with your wives in an understanding way, as with someone weaker, since she is a woman; and show her honor as a fellow heir of the grace of life, so that your prayers will not be hindered. (NASB)

8. **The husband must manage his own home well; he is the manager.**

   **1 Timothy 3:4** He must manage his own family well and see that his children obey him, and he must do so in a manner worthy of full respect. (NIV)

9. **The husband and father is primarily responsible for training the children.**

   **Ephesians 6:4** Fathers, do not provoke your children to anger, but bring them up in the discipline and instruction of the Lord. See also Training Children.

10. **God's design for the wife is that of a helper suitable for man.**

    **Genesis 2:18** Then the LORD God said, "It is not good that the man should be alone; I will make him a helper fit for him."

11. **Both husband and wife must seek to reflect the relationship between Christ and his church.**

    **Ephesians 5:25, 32**

12. **A wife is to submit to her husband, as the church submits to Christ.**

    **Ephesians 5:22–24** Wives, submit to your own husbands, as to the Lord. For the husband is head of the wife, as also Christ is head of the church; and He is the Savior of the body. Therefore, just as the church is subject to Christ, so let the wives be to their own husbands in everything. (NKJV)
    **Colossians 3:18** Wives, submit to your own husbands, as is fitting in the Lord. (NKJV)
    **1 Peter 3:1–2** Likewise, wives, be subject to your own husbands, so that even if some do not obey the word, they may be won without a word by the conduct of their wives—when they see your respectful and pure conduct.

13. **A woman is not to exercise authority over a man.**

    **1 Timothy 2:11–14** A woman should learn in quietness and full submission. I do not permit a woman to teach or to assume authority over a man; she must be quiet. For Adam was formed first, then Eve. And Adam was not the one deceived; it was the woman who was deceived and became a sinner. (NIV)

14. **The Bible gives a description of a wife of noble character, who uses her gifts faithfully.**

    **Proverbs 31:10–31**
    **Proverbs 31:10–11** Who can find a virtuous wife? For her worth is far above rubies. The heart of her husband safely trusts her; so he will have no lack of gain. (NKJV)

15. **The fear of the Lord is more important than physical beauty.**

    **Proverbs 31:30** Charm is deceitful, and beauty is vain, but a woman who fears the LORD is to be praised.
    **1 Peter 3:3–4** Do not let your adorning be external—the braiding of hair, the wearing of gold, or the putting on of clothing—but let your adorning be the hidden person of the heart with the imperishable beauty of a gentle and quiet spirit, which in God's sight is very precious.

16. **Husbands and wives must not fight and destroy each other.**

   Galatians 5:15 But if you bite and devour one another, beware lest you be consumed by one another! (NKJV)

17. **Both husband and wife must quickly pursue peace when trouble arises.**

   Matthew 5:23–24 So if you are offering your gift at the altar and there remember that your brother has something against you, leave your gift there before the altar and go. First be reconciled to your brother, and then come and offer your gift.

   Romans 12:18 If possible, so far as it depends on you, live peaceably with all.

18. **A house divided against itself cannot stand.**

   Matthew 12:25 Knowing their thoughts, he said to them, "Every kingdom divided against itself is laid waste, and no city or house divided against itself will stand."

19. **Keep loving those who are wayward.**

   2 Samuel 18:33 *(David never lost his love for his son Absalom, who tried to kill him. When he learned of his death, he wept.)* And the king was deeply moved and went up to the chamber over the gate and wept. And as he went, he said, "O my son Absalom, my son, my son Absalom! Would I had died instead of you, O Absalom, my son, my son!"

# Mixed Marriages

**1. Don't be yoked with an unbeliever.**

**2 Corinthians 6:14–16** Do not be yoked together with unbelievers. For what do righteousness and wickedness have in common? Or what fellowship can light have with darkness? What harmony is there between Christ and Belial? Or what does a believer have in common with an unbeliever? What agreement is there between the temple of God and idols? For we are the temple of the living God. As God has said: "I will live with them and walk among them, and I will be their God, and they will be my people." (NIV)

**2. Two cannot walk together unless they are agreed.**

**Amos 3:3** Do two walk together unless they have agreed to do so? (NIV)

**3. There were sad results of mixed marriages prior to the flood.**

**Genesis 6:1–4**

**4. God's people are warned against mixed marriages; unbelievers will lead them to sin.**

**Exodus 34:16** Then you will accept their daughters, who sacrifice to other gods, as wives for your sons. And they will seduce your sons to commit adultery against me by worshiping other gods. (NLT)

**Deuteronomy 7:3–4** You must not intermarry with them [the heathen]. Do not let your daughters and sons marry their sons and daughters, for they will lead your children away from me to worship other gods. Then the anger of the LORD will burn against you, and he will quickly destroy you. (NLT)

5. **God will reveal his anger if and when his people marry unbelievers.**

   **Joshua 23:12–13** For if you ever go back and cling to the rest of these nations, these which remain among you, and intermarry with them, so that you associate with them and they with you, know with certainty that the LORD your God will not continue to drive these nations out from before you; but they will be a snare and a trap to you, and a whip on your sides and thorns in your eyes, until you perish from off this good land which the LORD your God has given you. (NASB)

6. **In Ezra's time many did intermarry. This led to much sin, and Ezra confessed the guilt of God's people.**

   **Ezra 9:1–15**
   **Ezra 9:1–2** The princes approached me [Ezra], saying, "The people of Israel . . . have taken some of their daughters as wives for themselves and for their sons, so that the holy race has intermingled with the peoples of the lands; indeed, the hands of the princes and the rulers have been foremost in this unfaithfulness." (NASB)

7. **Men of Judah intermarried and were led into deep sin. God was angry with them.**

   **Nehemiah 13:23–27** In those days I also saw that the Jews had married women from Ashdod, Ammon and Moab. As for their children, half spoke in the language of Ashdod, and none of them was able to speak the language of Judah, but the language of his own people. So I contended with them and cursed them and struck some of them and pulled out their hair, and made them swear by God, "You shall not give your daughters to their sons, nor take of their daughters for your sons or for yourselves. Did not Solomon king of Israel sin regarding these things? Yet among the many nations there was no king like him, and he was loved by his God, and God made him king over all Israel; nevertheless the foreign women caused even him to sin. Do we then hear about you that you have committed all this great evil by acting unfaithfully against our God by marrying foreign women?" (NASB)

# Obedience, Keeping the Commandments

1. Jesus requires obedience.

   John 14:15 If you love Me, you will keep My commandments. (NASB)

2. Keeping the commandments of Jesus brings joy; you will remain in his love.

   John 15:10–17

3. Stay on the straight and narrow path that leads to life; the broad path leads to death.

   Matthew 7:13–14 Enter through the narrow gate; for the gate is wide and the way is broad that leads to destruction, and there are many who enter through it. For the gate is small and the way is narrow that leads to life, and there are few who find it. (NASB)

4. Not all who say, "Lord, Lord," will enter God's kingdom.

   Matthew 7:21 Not everyone who says to Me, "Lord, Lord," will enter the kingdom of heaven, but he who does the will of My Father who is in heaven will enter. (NASB)

5. Jesus gave us the parable of the wise and foolish builders.

   Matthew 7:24–27

6. God rewards obedience.

   Proverbs 13:13 Whoever scorns instruction will pay for it, but whoever respects a command is rewarded. (NIV)

7. To obey is better than sacrifice.

1 Samuel 15:22–23 Samuel said, "Has the LORD as much delight in burnt offerings and sacrifices as in obeying the voice of the LORD? Behold, to obey is better than sacrifice, and to heed than the fat of rams. For rebellion is as the sin of divination, and insubordination is as iniquity and idolatry. Because you have rejected the word of the LORD, He has also rejected you from being king." (NASB)

8. Listen to God's Word and do what it says.

Luke 11:28 But He said, "On the contrary, blessed are those who hear the word of God and observe it." (NASB)
James 1:22–25; 2:14–26

9. To love God is to keep his commandments.

1 John 5:2–3 By this we know that we love the children of God, when we love God and observe His commandments. For this is the love of God, that we keep His commandments; and His commandments are not burdensome. (NASB)

10. God's blessing and favor rest on those who obey him; obedience is the way to joy and peace.

Psalm 1
Psalm 19:7–14
Psalm 119:1–8

11. If you truly know and love the Lord, you will want to keep his commands.

1 John 2:3–6 By this we know that we have come to know Him, if we keep His commandments. The one who says, "I have come to know Him," and does not keep His commandments, is a liar, and the truth is not in him; but whoever keeps His word, in him the love of God has truly been perfected. By this we know that we are in Him: the one who says he abides in Him ought himself to walk in the same manner as He walked. (NASB)
1 John 5:2–4 By this we know that we love the children of God, when we love God and observe His commandments. For

this is the love of God, that we keep His commandments; and His commandments are not burdensome. For whatever is born of God overcomes the world; and this is the victory that has overcome the world—our faith. (NASB)

2 John 6 And this is love, that we walk according to His commandments. This is the commandment, just as you have heard from the beginning, that you should walk in it. (NASB)

12. **God teaches you the way to go, what is best for you, the way to peace.**

Isaiah 48:17–19 This is what the LORD says—your Redeemer, the Holy One of Israel: "I am the LORD your God, who teaches you what is good for you and leads you along the paths you should follow. Oh, that you had listened to my commands! Then you would have had peace flowing like a gentle river and righteousness rolling over you like waves in the sea. Your descendants would have been like the sands along the seashore—too many to count! There would have been no need for your destruction, or for cutting off your family name." (NLT)

13. **God's promises should motivate us to live a life of purity and holiness.**

2 Corinthians 7:1 Since we have these promises, beloved, let us cleanse ourselves from every defilement of body and spirit, bringing holiness to completion in the fear of God.

14. **Use your freedom in Christ, not to do evil but to serve him.**

Galatians 5:13 For you were called to freedom, brothers. Only do not use your freedom as an opportunity for the flesh, but through love serve one another.

15. **Swerve neither to the left nor to the right of the pathway of obedience.**

Proverbs 4:25–27 Let your eyes look straight ahead; fix your gaze directly before you. Give careful thought to the paths for your feet and be steadfast in all your ways. Do not turn to the right or the left; keep your foot from evil. (NIV)

# Overcoming Evil

*How to Handle It When Others Wrong You*

1. **Seek to communicate privately with the person who has wronged you.**

    **Matthew 18:15** If your brother or sister sins, go and point out their fault, just between the two of you. If they listen to you, you have won them over. (NIV)

2. **If you can't get the matter settled, take one or two with you.**

    **Matthew 18:16** But if they will not listen, take one or two others along, so that "every matter may be established by the testimony of two or three witnesses." (NIV)

3. **If that doesn't work, tell it to the church; seek help there.**

    **Matthew 18:17** If they still refuse to listen, tell it to the church; and if they refuse to listen even to the church, treat them as you would a pagan or a tax collector. (NIV)

4. **Bless those who persecute you.**

    **Romans 12:14** Bless those who persecute you; bless and do not curse. (NIV)

5. **Paul tells how to overcome evil and how to react when someone wrongs you.**

    **Romans 12:17–21**

**6. Do not seek revenge.**

**Romans 12:17** Repay no one evil for evil, but give thought to do what is honorable in the sight of all.

**Romans 12:19** Beloved, never avenge yourselves, but leave it to the wrath of God, for it is written, "Vengeance is mine, I will repay, says the Lord."

**Proverbs 20:22** Do not say, "I will repay evil"; wait for the Lord, and he will deliver you.

**7. Pursue peace with everyone.**

**Romans 12:18** If possible, so far as it depends on you, live peaceably with all.

**8. Overcome evil with good.**

**Romans 12:21** Do not be overcome by evil, but overcome evil with good.

**9. Imitate Jesus by suffering wrongfully, if need be; in no way should you try to get even.**

1 Peter 2:18–23

**1 Peter 2:19–23** For this is a gracious thing, when, mindful of God, one endures sorrows while suffering unjustly. For what credit is it if, when you sin and are beaten for it, you endure? But if when you do good and suffer for it you endure, this is a gracious thing in the sight of God. For to this you have been called, because Christ also suffered for you, leaving you an example, so that you might follow in his steps. He committed no sin, neither was deceit found in his mouth. When he was reviled, he did not revile in return; when he suffered, he did not threaten, but continued entrusting himself to him who judges justly.

**1 Peter 3:8–9** Finally, all of you, have unity of mind, sympathy, brotherly love, a tender heart, and a humble mind. Do not repay evil for evil or reviling for reviling, but on the contrary, bless, for to this you were called, that you may obtain a blessing.

10. Love your enemies and do good to them.

> Matthew 5:43–47
>
> Romans 12:20 If your enemy is hungry, feed him; if he is thirsty, give him something to drink. In doing this, you will heap burning coals on his head. (NIV)

11. Turn the other cheek; be kind to the person who has wronged you.

> Matthew 5:38–42
>
> 1 Thessalonians 5:15 Make sure that nobody pays back wrong for wrong, but always strive to do what is good for each other and for everyone else. (NIV)

12. Do not testify against your neighbor, nor seek revenge.

> Proverbs 24:28–29 Be not a witness against your neighbor without cause, and do not deceive with your lips. Do not say, "I will do to him as he has done to me; I will pay the man back for what he has done."

13. Moses gives a practical example of what to do after someone has wronged you.

> Exodus 23:4–5 If you meet your enemy's ox or his donkey going astray, you shall bring it back to him. If you see the donkey of one who hates you lying down under its burden, you shall refrain from leaving him with it; you shall rescue it with him.

# Overcoming Sin, Changing

## *To Please God and Resolve Problems*

*See also* Progressive Sanctification, Repentance

1. **True Christians can change, for God makes it possible through a spiritual renewal.**

   **2 Corinthians 5:17** Therefore, if anyone is in Christ, he is a new creation. The old has passed away; behold, the new has come.

   **Ezekiel 36:25–27** I will sprinkle clean water on you, and you shall be clean from all your uncleannesses, and from all your idols I will cleanse you. And I will give you a new heart, and a new spirit I will put within you. And I will remove the heart of stone from your flesh and give you a heart of flesh. And I will put my Spirit within you, and cause you to walk in my statutes and be careful to obey my rules.

2. **Believers are children of God, born again by the Holy Spirit.**

   **John 1:12–13** But to all who believed him and accepted him, he gave the right to become children of God. They are reborn—not with a physical birth resulting from human passion or plan, but a birth that comes from God. (NLT)

   **Titus 3:4–7** But—When God our Savior revealed his kindness and love, he saved us, not because of the righteous things we had done, but because of his mercy. He washed away our sins, giving us a new birth and new life through the Holy Spirit. He generously poured out the Spirit upon us through Jesus Christ our Savior. (NLT)

3. All Christians are called to live by the Holy Spirit, who dwells in us and empowers us to overcome sin and lead a godly life.

Romans 8:1–14

Romans 8:9 However, you are not in the flesh but in the Spirit, if indeed the Spirit of God dwells in you. But if anyone does not have the Spirit of Christ, he does not belong to Him. (NASB)

Romans 8:13–14 For if you are living according to the flesh, you must die; but if by the Spirit you are putting to death the deeds of the body, you will live. For all who are being led by the Spirit of God, these are sons of God. (NASB)

4. God calls us to work out our salvation in every area of life. We need not do it on our own. God enables us to do so.

Philippians 2:12–13 So then, my beloved, just as you have always obeyed, not as in my presence only, but now much more in my absence, work out your salvation with fear and trembling; for it is God who is at work in you, both to will and to work for His good pleasure. (NASB)

5. God has given us all we need for life and godliness.

2 Peter 1:3 His divine power has given us everything we need for a godly life through our knowledge of him who called us by his own glory and goodness. (NIV)

6. God will make all grace abound to you, so that you can overcome any specific sin and do his will.

2 Corinthians 9:8 And God is able to bless you abundantly, so that in all things at all times, having all that you need, you will abound in every good work. (NIV)

7. A true Christian will not continue to live in sin.

1 John 3:4–10

1 John 3:6 No one who lives in him keeps on sinning. No one who continues to sin has either seen him or known him. (NIV)

1 John 3:9 No one who is born of God will continue to sin, because God's seed remains in them; they cannot go on sinning, because they have been born of God. (NIV)

8. By nature we are slaves to sin. Jesus came to set us free.

John 8:31–36

John 8:34–36 Jesus answered them, "Truly, truly, I say to you, everyone who commits sin is a slave to sin. The slave does not remain in the house forever; the son remains forever. So if the Son sets you free, you will be free indeed."

9. Christians are set free so that we may be slaves to righteousness.

Romans 6:15–18 What then? Are we to sin because we are not under law but under grace? By no means! Do you not know that if you present yourselves to anyone as obedient slaves, you are slaves of the one whom you obey, either of sin, which leads to death, or of obedience, which leads to righteousness? But thanks be to God, that you who were once slaves of sin have become obedient from the heart to the standard of teaching to which you were committed, and, having been set free from sin, have become slaves of righteousness.

10. We must keep working to overcome sin and use our bodies to serve the Lord only.

Romans 6:19–23

11. In response to God's saving grace keep putting off old sinful ways and putting on new and godly ways.

Ephesians 4:22–24 Throw off your old sinful nature and your former way of life, which is corrupted by lust and deception. Instead, let the Spirit renew your thoughts and attitudes. Put on your new nature, created to be like God—truly righteous and holy. (NLT)

12. The apostle Paul gives us specific instructions on what must be done.

    Ephesians 4:25–5:21
    Colossians 3:1–17

13. We are directed to live by the Spirit and put off the acts of the sinful nature and seek the fruit of the Spirit.

    Galatians 5:16–26
    Galatians 5:19–26 Now the works of the flesh are evident: sexual immorality, impurity, sensuality, idolatry, sorcery, enmity, strife, jealousy, fits of anger, rivalries, dissensions, divisions, envy, drunkenness, orgies, and things like these. I warn you, as I warned you before, that those who do such things will not inherit the kingdom of God. But the fruit of the Spirit is love, joy, peace, patience, kindness, goodness, faithfulness, gentleness, self-control; against such things there is no law. And those who belong to Christ Jesus have crucified the flesh with its passions and desires. If we live by the Spirit, let us also walk by the Spirit. Let us not become conceited, provoking one another, envying one another.

14. **Adulterers, drunkards, homosexuals and others regarded by many as having incurable diseases can by God's power and grace overcome their sin.**

    1 Corinthians 6:9–11 Do you not know that the unrighteous will not inherit the kingdom of God? Do not be deceived: neither the sexually immoral, nor idolaters, nor adulterers, nor men who practice homosexuality, nor thieves, nor the greedy, nor drunkards, nor revilers, nor swindlers will inherit the kingdom of God. And such were some of you. But you were washed, you were sanctified, you were justified in the name of the Lord Jesus Christ and by the Spirit of our God.

15. Do not allow yourself to be mastered by any sin.

    1 Corinthians 6:12 "I have the right to do anything," you say—but not everything is beneficial. "I have the right to do anything"—but I will not be mastered by anything. (NIV)

**2 Peter 2:19** They [false teachers] promise them freedom, while they themselves are slaves of depravity—for "people are slaves to whatever has mastered them." (NIV)

16. **Use the whole armor of God as you fight the spiritual battle.**

    **Ephesians 6:10–18**
    **Ephesians 6:10–11** Finally, be strong in the Lord and in the strength of His might. Put on the full armor of God, so that you will be able to stand firm against the schemes of the devil. (NASB)

17. **Be vigilant! Your adversary, the devil, would like to devour you.**

    **1 Peter 5:8–9** Be of sober spirit, be on the alert. Your adversary, the devil, prowls around like a roaring lion, seeking someone to devour. But resist him, firm in your faith, knowing that the same experiences of suffering are being accomplished by your brethren who are in the world. (NASB)

18. **Resist the devil, who wants to keep you in bondage to sin.**

    **James 4:17** Therefore, to one who knows the right thing to do and does not do it, to him it is sin. (NASB)

19. **The devil may get others to entice you. If and when this happens, resolutely refuse to consent.**

    **Proverbs 1:10–19**
    **Proverbs 1:10** My son, if sinful men entice you, do not give in to them. (NIV)

20. **Stand firm; don't vacillate; don't be moved.**

    **1 Corinthians 15:58** Therefore, my dear brothers and sisters, stand firm. Let nothing move you. Always give yourselves fully to the work of the Lord, because you know that your labor in the Lord is not in vain. (NIV)

21. Studiously avoid the path of the wicked; turn from it.

    **Proverbs 4:14–15** Do not enter the path of the wicked and do not proceed in the way of evil men. Avoid it, do not pass by it; turn away from it and pass on. (NASB)

22. Pray earnestly, fervently for God to give you victory over sinful thoughts, words and deeds, as did the psalmist.

    **Psalm 19:12–14** How can I know all the sins lurking in my heart? Cleanse me from these hidden faults. Keep your servant from deliberate sins! Don't let them control me. Then I will be free of guilt and innocent of great sin. May the words of my mouth and the meditation of my heart be pleasing to you, O Lord, my rock and my redeemer. (NLT)

# Peace, Rest

*See also* Conscience

1. **Christ gives peace and rest to all who come to him in faith.**

   **Matthew 11:28–30** Come to me, all you who are weary and burdened, and I will give you rest. Take my yoke upon you and learn from me, for I am gentle and humble in heart, and you will find rest for your souls. For my yoke is easy and my burden is light. (NIV)

2. **Peace comes through justification by faith in Jesus.**

   **Romans 5:1** Since we have been justified through faith, we have peace with God through our Lord Jesus Christ. (NIV)

3. **Jesus gives us peace.**

   **John 14:27** Peace I leave with you; my peace I give you. I do not give to you as the world gives. Do not let your hearts be troubled and do not be afraid. (NIV)

4. **Jesus was punished for our sins so that we may have peace.**

   **Isaiah 53:5** The punishment that brought us peace was on him, and by his wounds we are healed. (NIV)

5. **The penitent woman, who wept at Jesus' feet, found peace through him.**

   **Luke 7:36–50**
   **Luke 7:48** Then Jesus said to her, "Your sins are forgiven." (NIV)
   **Luke 7:50** Jesus said to the woman, "Your faith has saved you; go in peace." (NIV)

6. Humble trust in the Lord gives peace.

Psalm 4:8 I will both lie down in peace, and sleep; for You alone, O LORD, make me dwell in safety. (NKJV)

7. God promises peace to his people.

Psalm 85:8 I will hear what God the LORD will speak, for He will speak peace to His people and to His saints; but let them not turn back to folly. (NKJV)

8. Peace is the result of being controlled by the Spirit.

Romans 8:6 So letting your sinful nature control your mind leads to death. But letting the Spirit control your mind leads to life and peace. (NLT)

9. Peace is the fruit of the Spirit.

Galatians 5:22–23 But the Holy Spirit produces this kind of fruit in our lives: love, joy, peace, patience, kindness, goodness, faithfulness, gentleness, and self-control. (NLT)

10. God gives peace to those whose minds are fixed on him.

Isaiah 26:3–4 You will keep him in perfect peace, whose mind is stayed on You, because he trusts in You. Trust in the LORD forever, for in Yah, the LORD, is everlasting strength. (NKJV)

11. The peace of God comes through praying in faith.

Philippians 4:6–7 Don't worry about anything; instead, pray about everything. Tell God what you need, and thank him for all he has done. Then you will experience God's peace, which exceeds anything we can understand. His peace will guard your hearts and minds as you live in Christ Jesus. (NLT)

12. Jesus is the Prince of Peace.

Isaiah 9:6 And he will be called: Wonderful Counselor, Mighty God, Everlasting Father, Prince of Peace. (NLT)

13. Those who walk uprightly enter into peace.

   Isaiah 57:2 For those who follow godly paths will rest in peace when they die. (NLT)

14. God revives, heals, and gives peace to those who are contrite.

   Isaiah 57:14–21
   Isaiah 57:19–20 "Peace, peace to him who is far off and to him who is near," says the LORD, "and I will heal him." But the wicked are like the troubled sea, when it cannot rest, whose waters cast up mire and dirt. (NKJV)

15. There is no peace for the wicked.

   Isaiah 57:21 "There is no peace," says my God, "for the wicked." (NKJV)

16. False prophets will say, "Peace, peace," when there is no peace.

   Jeremiah 8:11–12 They have healed the wound of my people lightly, saying, "Peace, peace," when there is no peace. Were they ashamed when they committed abomination? No, they were not at all ashamed; they did not know how to blush. Therefore they shall fall among the fallen; when I punish them, they shall be overthrown, says the LORD.

# Peacemakers, Peacekeepers

*See also* Forgiving Others

Note: Texts are listed which give instructions concerning peacemakers, peacekeeping, and promoting peace, harmony, and unity. It is important to remember that living by these instructions begins in the home and among extended family members.

1. **Jesus declares peacemakers to be blessed.**

   **Matthew 5:9** Blessed are the peacemakers, for they shall be called sons of God.

2. **Make every effort, do all you can, to live at peace with everyone.**

   **Hebrews 12:14** Strive for peace with everyone, and for the holiness without which no one will see the Lord.

   **Romans 12:18** If possible, so far as it depends on you, live peaceably with all.

3. **Seek peace and pursue it, speaking no evil or lies.**

   **Psalm 34:13–14** Keep your tongue from evil and your lips from speaking deceit. Turn away from evil and do good; seek peace and pursue it.

4. **Wisdom from God is peace loving.**

   **James 3:17–18** But the wisdom from above is first of all pure. It is also peace loving, gentle at all times, and willing to yield to others. It is full of mercy and good deeds. It shows no favoritism and is always sincere. And those who are peacemakers will plant seeds of peace and reap a harvest of righteousness. (NLT)

5. **Aim for perfection, be of one mind, live in peace.**

   2 Corinthians 13:11 Finally, brothers, rejoice. Aim for restoration, comfort one another, agree with one another, live in peace; and the God of love and peace will be with you.

6. **God takes delight in seeing his children living together in unity.**

   Psalm 133:1–3
   Psalm 133:1 How good and pleasant it is when God's people live together in unity! (NIV)

7. **If someone has something against you and your relationship is strained or broken, you must take the initiative to become reconciled. It is even more urgent than being in church on Sunday.**

   Matthew 5:23–24 So if you are presenting a sacrifice at the altar in the Temple and you suddenly remember that someone has something against you, leave your sacrifice there at the altar. Go and be reconciled to that person. Then come and offer your sacrifice to God. (NLT)

8. **If someone has sinned against you, you must take the initiative to get the matter cleared up, to restore peace.**

   Matthew 18:15 If another believer sins against you, go privately and point out the offense. If the other person listens and confesses it, you have won that person back. (NLT)

9. **If that person will not listen to you, seek the help of one or two other believers.**

   Matthew 18:16 But if you are unsuccessful, take one or two others with you and go back again, so that everything you say may be confirmed by two or three witnesses. (NLT)

10. **If he will not listen to them, tell it to the church.**

   Matthew 18:17 If the person still refuses to listen, take your case to the church. Then if he or she won't accept the church's decision, treat that person as a pagan or a corrupt tax collector. (NLT)

11. **To promote peace, harmony, and unity, love one another from the heart. Overlook many offenses, sins.**

   1 Peter 1:22–23 You were cleansed from your sins when you obeyed the truth, so now you must show sincere love to each other as brothers and sisters. Love each other deeply with all your heart. For you have been born again, but not to a life that will quickly end. Your new life will last forever because it comes from the eternal, living word of God. (NLT)

   1 Peter 4:8 Most important of all, continue to show deep love for each other, for love covers a multitude of sins. (NLT)

12. **Peter gives other ways by which we can promote peace and harmony.**

   1 Peter 3:8–11 Finally, all of you, have unity of mind, sympathy, brotherly love, a tender heart, and a humble mind. Do not repay evil for evil or reviling for reviling, but on the contrary, bless, for to this you were called, that you may obtain a blessing. For "Whoever desires to love life and see good days, let him keep his tongue from evil and his lips from speaking deceit; let him turn away from evil and do good; let him seek peace and pursue it."

13. **Use your God-given freedom to serve one another and avoid bitter strife.**

   Galatians 5:13–15 For you were called to freedom, brothers. Only do not use your freedom as an opportunity for the flesh, but through love serve one another. For the whole law is fulfilled in one word: "You shall love your neighbor as yourself." But if you bite and devour one another, watch out that you are not consumed by one another.

14. **Put off the deeds of the sinful nature which destroy peace and harmony.**

   Galatians 5:19–20 Now the works of the flesh are evident: sexual immorality, impurity, sensuality, idolatry, sorcery, enmity, strife, jealousy, fits of anger, rivalries, dissensions, divisions.

**Galatians 5:22–23** But the fruit of the Spirit is love, joy, peace, patience, kindness, goodness, faithfulness, gentleness, self-control; against such things there is no law.

15. **Follow the golden rule given by Jesus.**

**Matthew 7:12** So whatever you wish that others would do to you, do also to them, for this is the Law and the Prophets.

16. **Be patient. Bear with one another.**

**Proverbs 15:18** A hot-tempered man stirs up strife, but the slow to anger calms a dispute. (NASB)

**Proverbs 20:3** Keeping away from strife is an honor for a man, but any fool will quarrel. (NASB)

**Proverbs 26:21** Like charcoal to hot embers and wood to fire, so is a contentious man to kindle strife. (NASB)

**1 Corinthians 13:4** Love is patient, love is kind and is not jealous; love does not brag and is not arrogant. (NASB)

17. **An angry person causes dissension.**

**Proverbs 29:22** An angry person stirs up conflict, and a hot-tempered person commits many sins. (NIV)

18. **Stirring up another person's anger also produces strife.**

**Proverbs 30:33** For as churning cream produces butter, and as twisting the nose produces blood, so stirring up anger produces strife. (NIV)

19. **Put on other Christ-like virtues which promote peace.**

**Colossians 3:12–13** Since God chose you to be the holy people he loves, you must clothe yourselves with tenderhearted mercy, kindness, humility, gentleness, and patience. Make allowance for each other's faults, and forgive anyone who offends you. Remember, the Lord forgave you, so you must forgive others. (NLT)

20. **Peacefully accept God-ordained diversity within basic unity.**

    **Ephesians 4:1–16**

    **Ephesians 4:2–4** . . . with all humility and gentleness, with patience, bearing with one another in love, eager to maintain the unity of the Spirit in the bond of peace. There is one body and one Spirit—just as you were called to the one hope that belongs to your call.

21. **Avoid judging one another in disputable matters.**

    **Romans 14:1–23**

    **Romans 14:1** As for the one who is weak in faith, welcome him, but not to quarrel over opinions.

    **Romans 14:19** So then let us pursue what makes for peace and for mutual upbuilding.

22. **Communicate in a manner that promotes peace.**

    **Ephesians 4:15** Rather, speaking the truth in love, we are to grow up in every way into him who is the head, into Christ.

    **Ephesians 4:29** Let no corrupting talk come out of your mouths, but only such as is good for building up, as fits the occasion, that it may give grace to those who hear.

23. **Accept others in the spirit of unity even while you strongly disagree with them on disputable matters. The primary goal is to glorify the Lord.**

    **Romans 15:5–7** May God, who gives this patience and encouragement, help you live in complete harmony with each other, as is fitting for followers of Christ Jesus. Then all of you can join together with one voice, giving praise and glory to God, the Father of our Lord Jesus Christ. Therefore, accept each other just as Christ has accepted you so that God will be given glory. (NLT)

24. **If a legal dispute develops between you and another Christian, do not turn to unbelievers for help. Rather seek the help of one or more fellow Christians.**

    **1 Corinthians 6:1–8**

1 Corinthians 6:1 When one of you has a dispute with another believer, how dare you file a lawsuit and ask a secular court to decide the matter instead of taking it to other believers! (NLT)
1 Corinthians 6:4–6 If you have legal disputes about such matters, why go to outside judges who are not respected by the church? I am saying this to shame you. Isn't there anyone in all the church who is wise enough to decide these issues? But instead, one believer sues another—right in front of unbelievers! (NLT)

25. Be willing to suffer wrongfully rather than to take another Christian to court.

1 Corinthians 6:7 Even to have such lawsuits with one another is a defeat for you. Why not just accept the injustice and leave it at that? Why not let yourselves be cheated? (NLT)

26. Get rid of those traits that cause enmity and dissension.

Ephesians 4:31 Get rid of all bitterness, rage and anger, brawling and slander, along with every form of malice. (NIV)

27. Forgive those who have sinned against you. Forgive as God forgave you. That is, in the manner God forgave you. Imitate God in forgiving others. There is no peace, no reconciliation apart from forgiveness.

Ephesians 4:32 Be kind and compassionate to one another, forgiving each other, just as in Christ God forgave you. (NIV)
Ephesians 5:1–2 Follow God's example, therefore, as dearly loved children and walk in the way of love, just as Christ loved us and gave himself up for us as a fragrant offering and sacrifice to God. (NIV)

159

# Persecution

Note: Suffering persecution is being maltreated by others because you are a true disciple of Christ. It includes being falsely accused, unjustly condemned or imprisoned, being ridiculed, scorned, rejected, or injured. Persecution is not suffering for doing wrong toward others or for disobeying rightful authority.

1. **Why do people persecute Christians, even when they are doing good?**

   **John 15:18–21** If the world hates you, know that it has hated me before it hated you. If you were of the world, the world would love you as its own; but because you are not of the world, but I chose you out of the world, therefore the world hates you. Remember the word that I said to you: "A servant is not greater than his master." If they persecuted me, they will also persecute you. If they kept my word, they will also keep yours. But all these things they will do to you on account of my name, because they do not know him who sent me.

   **2 Timothy 3:10–14** You, however, have followed my teaching, my conduct, my aim in life, my faith, my patience, my love, my steadfastness, my persecutions and sufferings that happened to me at Antioch, at Iconium, and at Lystra—which persecutions I endured; yet from them all the Lord rescued me. Indeed, all who desire to live a godly life in Christ Jesus will be persecuted, while evil people and impostors will go on from bad to worse, deceiving and being deceived. But as for you, continue in what you have learned and have firmly believed, knowing from whom you learned it.

   **1 John 3:1** See what great love the Father has lavished on us, that we should be called children of God! And that is what we are! The reason the world does not know us is that it did not know him. (NIV)

2. **Cain persecuted his brother Abel because his own works were evil, while Abel's were righteous.**

> Genesis 4:2–7
>
> 1 John 3:12–14 We should not be like Cain, who was of the evil one and murdered his brother. And why did he murder him? Because his own deeds were evil and his brother's righteous. Do not be surprised, brothers, that the world hates you. We know that we have passed out of death into life, because we love the brothers. Whoever does not love abides in death.

3. **Do good to and pray for those who persecute you. Love your enemies.**

> Matthew 5:38–42 You have heard that it was said, "An eye for an eye and a tooth for a tooth." But I say to you, do not resist the one who is evil. But if anyone slaps you on the right cheek, turn to him the other also. And if anyone would sue you and take your tunic, let him have your cloak as well. And if anyone forces you to go one mile, go with him two miles. Give to the one who begs from you, and do not refuse the one who would borrow from you.
>
> Matthew 5:43–48
>
> Matthew 5:43–45 You have heard that it was said, "You shall love your neighbor and hate your enemy." But I say to you, Love your enemies and pray for those who persecute you, so that you may be sons of your Father who is in heaven. For he makes his sun rise on the evil and on the good, and sends rain on the just and on the unjust.
>
> Romans 12:14 Bless those who persecute you; bless and do not curse them.

4. **Imitate Stephen, who prayed for his persecutors as they were stoning him.**

   **Acts 7:60** And falling to his knees he cried out with a loud voice, "Lord, do not hold this sin against them." And when he had said this, he fell asleep.

5. **In dealing with your persecutors be wise and innocent.**

   **Matthew 10:16** Behold, I am sending you out as sheep in the midst of wolves, so be wise as serpents and innocent as doves.

6. **If you are falsely accused, trust God to lead you.**

   **Matthew 10:17–20** Beware of men, for they will deliver you over to courts and flog you in their synagogues, and you will be dragged before governors and kings for my sake, to bear witness before them and the Gentiles. When they deliver you over, do not be anxious how you are to speak or what you are to say, for what you are to say will be given to you in that hour. For it is not you who speak, but the Spirit of your Father speaking through you.

7. **One need not get depressed due to severe persecution. Paul testifies to that.**

   **2 Corinthians 4:8–9** We are hard pressed on every side, but not crushed; perplexed, but not in despair; persecuted, but not abandoned; struck down, but not destroyed. (NIV)

   **2 Corinthians 11:23–29** *(Paul tells of the many things he suffered at the hands of his persecutors.)*

8. **Those who suffer for the sake of Christ will be blessed and should count it an honor to do so.**

   **1 Peter 4:12–16** Dear friends, do not be surprised at the fiery ordeal that has come on you to test you, as though something strange were happening to you. But rejoice inasmuch as you participate in the sufferings of Christ, so that you may be overjoyed when his glory is revealed. If you are insulted because of the name of Christ, you are blessed, for the Spirit of glory and of God rests on you. If you suffer, it should not be as a murderer or thief or any other kind of criminal, or even as a meddler. However, if you suffer as a Christian, do not be ashamed, but praise God that you bear that name. (NIV)

9. **Never be ashamed to be identified with those who are being persecuted. Rather, suffer with them, if need be.**

2 Timothy 1:8–9 Therefore do not be ashamed of the testimony about our Lord, nor of me his prisoner, but share in suffering for the gospel by the power of God, who saved us and called us to a holy calling, not because of our works but because of his own purpose and grace.

10. **Do not be ashamed of the gospel. Testify boldly and be ready to suffer persecution.**

2 Timothy 2:3 Share in suffering as a good soldier of Christ Jesus.

2 Timothy 2:8–10 Remember Jesus Christ, risen from the dead, the offspring of David, as preached in my gospel, for which I am suffering, bound with chains as a criminal. But the word of God is not bound! Therefore I endure everything for the sake of the elect, that they also may obtain the salvation that is in Christ Jesus with eternal glory.

11. **Do not be unsettled or let the devil lead you away from the faith through persecution.**

1 Thessalonians 3:2–4 We sent Timothy, our brother and God's coworker in the gospel of Christ, to establish and exhort you in your faith, that no one be moved by these afflictions. For you yourselves know that we are destined for this. For when we were with you, we kept telling you beforehand that we were to suffer affliction, just as it has come to pass, and just as you know.

12. **Jesus says that some do fall away when they are persecuted.**

Matthew 13:1–9 *(the parable of the sower)*
Matthew 13:18–23 *(Jesus interprets the parable.)*
Matthew 13:20–21 The seed falling on rocky ground refers to someone who hears the word and at once receives it with joy.

But since they have no root, they last only a short time. When trouble or persecution comes because of the word, they quickly fall away. (NIV)

13. **Some compromise the gospel to avoid persecution. Don't be like that.**

    **Galatians 6:12** Those who want to impress people by means of the flesh are trying to compel you to be circumcised. The only reason they do this is to avoid being persecuted for the cross of Christ. (NIV)

14. **Believers can keep God's Word when they are persecuted. David did.**

    **Psalm 119:51** The arrogant utterly deride me, yet I do not turn aside from Your law. (NASB)

    **Psalm 119:61** The cords of the wicked have encircled me, but I have not forgotten Your law. (NASB)

    **Psalm 119:69** The arrogant have forged a lie against me; with all my heart I will observe Your precepts. (NASB)

15. **If persecutors threaten you, obey God rather than man, as did Peter and John.**

    **Acts 4:18–20** And when they had summoned them, they commanded them not to speak or teach at all in the name of Jesus. But Peter and John answered and said to them, "Whether it is right in the sight of God to give heed to you rather than to God, you be the judge; for we cannot stop speaking about what we have seen and heard." (NASB)

    **Acts 5:17–32** *(The apostles went on preaching the gospel.)*

    **Acts 5:29** But Peter and the apostles answered, "We must obey God rather than men." (NASB)

    **Acts 5:41–42** So they went on their way from the presence of the Council, rejoicing that they had been considered worthy to suffer shame for His name. And every day, in the temple and from house to house, they kept right on teaching and preaching Jesus as the Christ. (NASB)

16. **Paul and Silas sang hymns while they were imprisoned.**

   **Acts 16:25** But about midnight Paul and Silas were praying and singing hymns of praise to God, and the prisoners were listening to them. (NASB)

17. **Paul was willing to die for the sake of Christ.**

   **Acts 21:12–13** When we heard this, we and the people there pleaded with Paul not to go up to Jerusalem. Then Paul answered, "Why are you weeping and breaking my heart? I am ready not only to be bound, but also to die in Jerusalem for the name of the Lord Jesus." (NIV)

18. **Those who are persecuted for righteousness' sake will be blessed.**

   **Matthew 5:10–12** Blessed are those who have been persecuted for the sake of righteousness, for theirs is the kingdom of heaven. Blessed are you when people insult you and persecute you, and falsely say all kinds of evil against you because of Me. Rejoice and be glad, for your reward in heaven is great; for in the same way they persecuted the prophets who were before you. (NASB)
   **2 Timothy 4:6–8** For I am already being poured out as a drink offering, and the time of my departure has come. I have fought the good fight, I have finished the course, I have kept the faith; in the future there is laid up for me the crown of righteousness, which the Lord, the righteous Judge, will award to me on that day; and not only to me, but also to all who have loved His appearing. (NASB)
   **Revelation 2:9–10** I know your afflictions and your poverty— yet you are rich! I know about the slander of those who say they are Jews and are not, but are a synagogue of Satan. Do not be afraid of what you are about to suffer. I tell you, the devil will put some of you in prison to test you, and you will suffer persecution for ten days. Be faithful, even to the point of death, and I will give you life as your victor's crown. (NIV)

19. **Hebrew Christians stood their ground under persecution and were rewarded for it.**

   **Hebrews 10:32–39**

Hebrews 10:33–35 Sometimes you were exposed to public ridicule and were beaten, and sometimes you helped others who were suffering the same things. You suffered along with those who were thrown into jail, and when all you owned was taken from you, you accepted it with joy. You knew there were better things waiting for you that will last forever. So do not throw away this confident trust in the Lord. Remember the great reward it brings you! (NLT)

20. **Be willing to suffer even for doing good.**

1 Peter 3:13–22

1 Peter 3:13–14 Who is going to harm you if you are eager to do good? But even if you should suffer for what is right, you are blessed. "Do not fear their threats; do not be frightened." (NIV)

1 Peter 3:17 It is better, if it is God's will, to suffer for doing good than for doing evil. (NIV)

21. **Unconverted sinners will at times heap abuse on you because you no longer join them in their sin.**

1 Peter 4:3–5 You have had enough in the past of the evil things that godless people enjoy—their immorality and lust, their feasting and drunkenness and wild parties, and their terrible worship of idols. Of course, your former friends are surprised when you no longer plunge into the flood of wild and destructive things they do. So they slander you. But remember that they will have to face God, who will judge everyone, both the living and the dead. (NLT)

22. **We who are saved by grace and through faith in Christ must also be willing and prepared to suffer for him.**

Philippians 1:27–30

Philippians 1:29–30 For you have been given not only the privilege of trusting in Christ but also the privilege of suffering for him. We are in this struggle together. You have seen my struggle in the past, and you know that I am still in the midst of it. (NLT)

23. How should you react when you are persecuted? See how Paul handled it.

1 Corinthians 4:9–13

1 Corinthians 4:11–13 To the present hour we hunger and thirst, we are poorly dressed and buffeted and homeless, and we labor, working with our own hands. When reviled, we bless; when persecuted, we endure; when slandered, we entreat. We have become, and are still, like the scum of the world, the refuse of all things.

# Prayer, Waiting on the Lord

*See also* **Trust**

1. **The Lord's Prayer is our model.**

   Matthew 6:9–13

2. **Pray "Our Father."**

   **Matthew 6:9** Pray then like this: "Our Father in heaven."

3. **Pray for daily needs.**

   **Matthew 6:11** "Give us this day our daily bread."

4. **Pray daily for the forgiveness of sins.**

   **Matthew 6:12** "And forgive us our debts, as we also have forgiven our debtors."

5. **We can approach God boldly through Jesus, our high priest, who understands our needs.**

   **Hebrews 4:14–16** So then, since we have a great High Priest who has entered heaven, Jesus the Son of God, let us hold firmly to what we believe. This High Priest of ours understands our weaknesses, for he faced all of the same testings we do, yet he did not sin. So let us come boldly to the throne of our gracious God. There we will receive his mercy, and we will find grace to help us when we need it most. (NLT)

6. **Cast all your anxiety on the Lord.**

   **1 Peter 5:6–7** So humble yourselves under the mighty power of God, and at the right time he will lift you up in honor. Give all your worries and cares to God, for he cares about you. (NLT)

7. **Pray about everything instead of worrying.**

   **Philippians 4:6–7** Don't worry about anything; instead, pray about everything. Tell God what you need, and thank him for all he has done. Then you will experience God's peace, which exceeds anything we can understand. His peace will guard your hearts and minds as you live in Christ Jesus. (NLT)

8. **Pray continually and give thanks in all circumstances.**

   **1 Thessalonians 5:17–18** Pray continually, give thanks in all circumstances; for this is God's will for you in Christ Jesus. (NIV)

9. **Pray in faith.**

   **James 1:6** But when you ask [for wisdom], you must believe and not doubt, because the one who doubts is like a wave of the sea, blown and tossed by the wind. (NIV)

10. **In time of sickness, pray.**

    James 5:14–16

11. **The prayer of a righteous person is powerful.**

    **James 5:16** Confess your sins to each other and pray for each other so that you may be healed. The prayer of a righteous man is powerful and effective. (NIV)

12. **Dare to pray for great things, as did Elijah.**

    **James 5:17–18** Elijah was a human being, even as we are. He prayed earnestly that it would not rain, and it did not rain on the land for three and a half years. Again he prayed, and the heavens gave rain, and the earth produced its crops. (NIV)

13. **God hears and answers prayer; he is near to his children.**

    **Psalm 34:15–18** The eyes of the LORD are on the righteous, and His ears are open to their cry. The face of the LORD is against those who do evil, to cut off the remembrance of them from the earth. The righteous cry out, and the LORD hears, and delivers them out of all their troubles. The LORD is near to those who have a broken heart, and saves such as have a contrite spirit. (NKJV)

14. **Pray and work, using the means available to you.**

    Nehemiah 4:9 But we prayed to our God, and because of them we set up a guard against them day and night. (NASB)

15. **In all your ways acknowledge the Lord.**

    Proverbs 3:5–6 Trust in the LORD with all your heart and do not lean on your own understanding. In all your ways acknowledge Him, and He will make your paths straight. (NASB)

16. **Seek the Lord while he may be found.**

    Isaiah 55:6 Seek the LORD while he may be found; call upon him while he is near.

17. **Thank God for his grace and mercy, praise him, and keep seeking his mercy.**

    Psalm 105:1–4

18. **Praise and thank God for answered prayer.**

    Psalm 66:13–20
    Psalm 66:17–20 I cried to him with my mouth, and high praise was on my tongue. If I had cherished iniquity in my heart, the Lord would not have listened. But truly God has listened; he has attended to the voice of my prayer. Blessed be God, because he has not rejected my prayer or removed his steadfast love from me!

19. **Pray for the forgiveness of sins.**

    Psalms 32 and 51
    Jeremiah 29:12–13 Then you will call on me and come and pray to me, and I will listen to you. You will seek me and find me when you seek me with all your heart. (NIV)
    Matthew 11:28–30 Come to me, all who labor and are heavy laden, and I will give you rest. Take my yoke upon you, and learn

from me, for I am gentle and lowly in heart, and you will find rest for your souls. For my yoke is easy, and my burden is light.
**Romans 10:13** For everyone who calls on the name of the Lord will be saved.
**1 John 1:7–9**
See also Forgiveness of Sins.

20. **Call on the Lord in time of trouble.**

    **Psalm 50:15** Call upon Me in the day of trouble; I will deliver you, and you shall glorify Me. (NKJV)

21. **Because Jesus was tried, as we are, he is able to help us.**

    **Hebrews 2:18** For because he himself has suffered when tempted, he is able to help those who are being tempted.
    **Hebrews 3:1** Therefore, holy brothers, you who share in a heavenly calling, consider Jesus, the apostle and high priest of our confession.

22. **God answers intercessory prayer.**

    **Acts 12:1–17** *(Peter was unjustly imprisoned. The church met for prayer. Peter was soon set free.)*
    **Acts 12:5** Peter was therefore kept in prison, but constant prayer was offered to God for him by the church. (NKJV)
    **Acts 12:12** So, when he had considered this [he realized that the angel had rescued him from prison], he came to the house of Mary, the mother of John whose surname was Mark, where many were gathered together praying. (NKJV)

# Progressive Sanctification
## *Growing in Faith and Godliness*

*See also* Overcoming Sin

1. **Keep growing in the grace and knowledge of Jesus Christ.**

   **2 Peter 3:18** But grow in the grace and knowledge of our Lord and Savior Jesus Christ. To him be the glory both now and to the day of eternity. Amen.

2. **Do not be content to be an immature Christian, as was the case with many Hebrew believers.**

   **Hebrews 5:11–6:4**
   **Hebrews 5:12–14** For though by this time you ought to be teachers, you need someone to teach you again the basic principles of the oracles of God. You need milk, not solid food, for everyone who lives on milk is unskilled in the word of righteousness, since he is a child. But solid food is for the mature, for those who have their powers of discernment trained by constant practice to distinguish good from evil.

3. **God works in us through his Word to bring us to spiritual maturity, to sanctify us.**

   **John 17:17** [*Jesus, thinking of his redeemed people, prayed,*] Sanctify them in the truth; Your word is truth. (NASB)
   **Colossians 3:16** Let the word of Christ richly dwell within you, with all wisdom teaching and admonishing one another with psalms and hymns and spiritual songs, singing with thankfulness in your hearts to God. (NASB)

1 Peter 2:2–3 Like newborn babies, long for the pure milk of the word, so that by it you may grow in respect to salvation, if you have tasted the kindness of the Lord. (NASB)

Psalm 119:11 Your word I have treasured in my heart, that I may not sin against You. (NASB)

Psalm 119:105 Your word is a lamp to my feet and a light to my path. (NASB)

4. The Bible, the inspired, inerrant Word of God, is that by which he trains us in righteousness so that we may be thoroughly equipped for every good work.

2 Timothy 3:16–17 All Scripture is inspired by God and profitable for teaching, for reproof, for correction, for training in righteousness; so that the man of God may be adequate, equipped for every good work. (NASB)

5. The Counselor, the Holy Spirit, teaches us through his own word.

John 14:25–26 I am telling you these things now while I am still with you. But when the Father sends the Advocate as my representative—that is, the Holy Spirit—he will teach you everything and will remind you of everything I have told you. (NLT)

6. The Word of God is immeasurably effective.

Hebrews 4:12 For the word of God is alive and powerful. It is sharper than the sharpest two-edged sword, cutting between soul and spirit, between joint and marrow. It exposes our innermost thoughts and desires. (NLT)

7. Like a runner in a race, keep pressing on until you have gained the victory, as did the apostle Paul.

Philippians 3:12–14 I don't mean to say that I have already achieved these things or that I have already reached perfection. But I press on to possess that perfection for which Christ Jesus first possessed me. No, dear brothers and sisters, I have not achieved it, but I focus on this one thing: Forgetting the past and looking forward to what lies ahead, I press on to reach the end of the race and receive the heavenly prize for which God, through Christ Jesus, is calling us. (NLT)

Note: Paul had a healthy dissatisfaction with himself, although he was already a mature Christian. He would neither focus on past failure, nor would he allow himself to become discouraged after he did fall. He kept pressing on.

8. **Get rid of everything that might hinder you and run the race with perseverance.**

    **Hebrews 12:1** Therefore we also, since we are surrounded by so great a cloud of witnesses, let us lay aside every weight, and the sin which so easily ensnares us, and let us run with endurance the race that is set before us. (NKJV)

9. **Fix your eyes on Jesus, the author and perfecter of your faith. Focus on all he did to save you!**

    **Hebrews 12:2** Looking unto Jesus, the author and finisher of our faith, who for the joy that was set before Him endured the cross, despising the shame, and has sat down at the right hand of the throne of God. (NKJV)

10. **Train yourself to be godly. Be like an athlete, who persists in training. That's what Paul counseled Timothy to do.**

    **1 Timothy 4:7–8** Do not waste time arguing over godless ideas and old wives' tales. Instead, train yourself to be godly. Physical training is good, but training for godliness is much better, promising benefits in this life and in the life to come. (NLT)

11. **Put much effort into living a godly life.**

    **2 Peter 3:14** Therefore, beloved, since you are waiting for these, be diligent to be found by him without spot or blemish, and at peace.

12. **Abide in Jesus Christ, the vine, through whom alone you can bear much fruit, to glorify God.**

    **John 15:1–8**

John 15:1 I am the true vine, and My Father is the vinedresser. (NKJV)

John 15:5 I am the vine, you are the branches. He who abides in Me, and I in him, bears much fruit; for without Me you can do nothing. (NKJV)

John 15:8 By this My Father is glorified, that you bear much fruit; so you will be my disciples. (NKJV)

13. Imitate Jesus so that you will become more and more Christ-like.

1 John 2:6 Whoever claims to live in him must live as Jesus did. (NIV)

For more on this see Imitating Jesus.

14. The apostle Peter lists some Christ-like virtues we should seek after.

2 Peter 1:5–9

2 Peter 1:5–7 For this very reason, make every effort to add to your faith goodness; and to goodness, knowledge; and to knowledge, self-control; and to self-control, perseverance; and to perseverance, godliness; and to godliness, mutual affection; and to mutual affection, love. (NIV)

15. We must be motivated to work at growing in faith and godliness by the victory we have through the suffering, death, and resurrection of Jesus Christ.

1 Corinthians 15:57–58 But thanks be to God! He gives us the victory through our Lord Jesus Christ. Therefore, my dear brothers and sisters, stand firm. Let nothing move you. Always give yourselves fully to the work of the Lord, because you know that your labor in the Lord is not in vain. (NIV)

2 Corinthians 7:1 Since we have these promises, dear friends, let us purify ourselves from everything that contaminates body and spirit, perfecting holiness out of reverence for God. (NIV)

Romans 12:1–2 Therefore, I urge you, brothers and sisters, in view of God's mercy [in giving you salvation], to offer your bodies as a living sacrifice, holy and pleasing to God—this is your true and proper worship. Do not conform to the pattern of this world, but be transformed by the renewing of your mind. Then you will be able to test and approve what God's will is—his good, pleasing and perfect will. (NIV)

16. **God uses his Word to revive the soul, make wise the simple, give joy to the heart, give light to the eyes, and much more.**

    **Psalm 19:7–11**
    **Psalm 19:7–8** The law of the LORD is perfect, converting the soul; the testimony of the LORD is sure, making wise the simple; the statutes of the LORD are right, rejoicing the heart; the commandment of the LORD is pure, enlightening the eyes. (NKJV)

17. **The Lord requires us to keep working out our salvation in every area of life, since he works in us by his Word and Spirit.**

    **Philippians 2:12–13** Therefore, my beloved, as you have always obeyed, not as in my presence only, but now much more in my absence, work out your own salvation with fear and trembling; for it is God who works in you both to will and to do for His good pleasure. (NKJV)

18. **God is graciously transforming every Christian more and more into the likeness of Jesus Christ.**

    **2 Corinthians 3:18** And we all, with unveiled face, beholding the glory of the Lord, are being transformed into the same image from one degree of glory to another. For this comes from the Lord who is the Spirit.

# Providence of God

*See also* Comfort, Trust

1. **God sovereignly works all things according to his will.**

   **Ephesians 1:10–11** In Him also we have obtained an inheritance, having been predestined according to His purpose who works all things after the counsel of His will. (NASB)

2. **God's sovereign rule extends over all things.**

   **Psalm 103:19** The LORD has established His throne in the heavens, and His sovereignty rules over all. (NASB)

   **Acts 17:28** For in Him we live and move and exist, as even some of your own poets have said, "For we also are His children." (NASB)

   **Romans 11:36** For from Him and through Him and to Him are all things. To Him be the glory forever. Amen. (NASB)

3. **God cares for the birds and the flowers and certainly will, then, care for his children.**

   **Matthew 6:25–34**

   **Matthew 6:26** Look at the birds. They don't plant or harvest or store food in barns, for your heavenly Father feeds them. And aren't you far more valuable to him than they are? (NLT)

   **Matthew 6:30** And if God cares so wonderfully for wildflowers that are here today and thrown into the fire tomorrow, he will certainly care for you. Why do you have so little faith? (NLT)

4. **God controls all the forces of nature and provides for all his creatures, especially his children.**

   **Psalm 104; Psalm 145; Psalm 147**

5. **God used ravens to care for Elijah.**

   **1 Kings 17:1–6**
   **1 Kings 17:4–5** "Drink from the brook and eat what the ravens bring you, for I have commanded them to bring you food." So Elijah did as the LORD told him and camped beside Kerith Brook, east of the Jordan. (NLT)

6. **By sending his people manna from heaven each day, God revealed his faithfulness, power, and love.**

   **Exodus 16**

7. **God is the potter, we are the clay. Be submissive to him.**

   **Jeremiah 18:1–10**
   **Jeremiah 18:5–6** Then the LORD gave me this message: "O Israel, can I not do to you as this potter has done to his clay? As the clay is in the potter's hand, so are you in my hand." (NLT)
   **Isaiah 45:9–13**
   **Isaiah 45:9–11** What sorrow awaits those who argue with their Creator. Does a clay pot argue with its maker? Does the clay dispute with the one who shapes it, saying, "Stop, you're doing it wrong!" Does the pot exclaim, "How clumsy can you be?" How terrible it would be if a newborn baby said to its father, "Why was I born?" or if it said to its mother, "Why did you make me this way?" This is what the LORD says—the Holy One of Israel and your Creator: "Do you question what I do for my children? Do you give me orders about the work of my hands?" (NLT)

8. **God uses wicked rulers to fulfill his purposes for his children.**

   **Isaiah 45:12–13** I am the one who made the earth and created people to live on it. With my hands I stretched out the heavens. All the stars are at my command. I will raise up Cyrus to fulfill my righteous purpose, and I will guide his actions. He will restore my city and free my captive people— without seeking a reward! I, the LORD of Heaven's Armies, have spoken! (NLT)
   **Ezra 7:1–10** *(God moved King Artaxerxes to give Ezra what he asked for, because "the hand of the LORD his God was on him.")*

Ezra 7:6 This Ezra went up from Babylon, and he was a scribe skilled in the law of Moses, which the LORD God of Israel had given; and the king granted him all he requested because the hand of the LORD his God was upon him. (NASB)

Ezra 7:10 This was because Ezra had determined to study and obey the Law of the LORD and to teach those decrees and regulations to the people of Israel. (NLT)

9. **God blesses those who by faith take refuge in him.**

Ruth *(The whole Book of Ruth reveals this very beautifully.)*
Ruth 2:11–12 Boaz replied . . . "May the LORD reward your work, and your wages be full from the LORD, the God of Israel, under whose wings you have come to seek refuge." (NASB)

Ruth 2:20 *(After Ruth had gleaned in Boaz's field, Naomi praised him.)* Naomi said to her daughter-in-law, "May he be blessed of the LORD who has not withdrawn his kindness to the living and to the dead." Again Naomi said to her, "The man is our relative, he is one of our closest relatives." (NASB)

10. **Not one of God's promises goes unfulfilled.**

Joshua 23:14 Now behold, today I am going the way of all the earth, and you know in all your hearts and in all your souls that not one word of all the good words which the LORD your God spoke concerning you has failed; all have been fulfilled for you, not one of them has failed. (NASB)

11. **God will also carry out his threats.**

Joshua 23:15–16 It shall come about that just as all the good words which the LORD your God spoke to you have come upon you, so the LORD will bring upon you all the threats, until He has destroyed you from off this good land which the LORD your God has given you. When you transgress the covenant of the LORD your God, which He commanded you, and go and serve other gods and bow down to them, then the anger of the LORD will burn against you, and you will perish quickly from off the good land which He has given you. (NASB)

12. **God used Gideon's small band to defeat Israel's enemies.**

Judges 7:1–25

Judges 7:2–3 The LORD said to Gideon, "The people who are with you are too many for me to give Midian into their hands, for Israel would become boastful, saying, 'My own power has delivered me.' Now therefore come, proclaim in the hearing of the people, saying, 'Whoever is afraid and trembling, let him return and depart from Mount Gilead.'" So 22,000 people returned, but 10,000 remained. (NASB)

13. **God promises to go with those to whom he gives a difficult task.**

Deuteronomy 31:7–8 Then Moses called to Joshua and said to him in the sight of all Israel, "Be strong and courageous, for you shall go with this people into the land which the LORD has sworn to their fathers to give them, and you shall give it to them as an inheritance. The LORD is the one who goes ahead of you; He will be with you. He will not fail you or forsake you. Do not fear or be dismayed." (NASB)

14. **Joseph acknowledged God's providence in being sold into slavery.**

Genesis 45:1–14 *(Joseph made himself known to his brothers.)*
Genesis 45:4–8 Then Joseph said to his brothers, "Please come closer to me." And they came closer. And he said, "I am your brother Joseph, whom you sold into Egypt. Now do not be grieved or angry with yourselves, because you sold me here, for God sent me before you to preserve life. For the famine has been in the land these two years, and there are still five years in which there will be neither plowing nor harvesting. God sent me before you to preserve for you a remnant in the earth, and to keep you alive by a great deliverance. Now, therefore, it was not you who sent me here, but God; and He has made me a father to Pharaoh and lord of all his household and ruler over all the land of Egypt. (NASB)
Genesis 50:15–21 *(Joseph reassured his brothers of his forgiveness toward them.)*
Genesis 50:19–21 But Joseph said to them, "Do not be afraid, for am I in God's place? As for you, you meant evil against me, but

God meant it for good in order to bring about this present result, to preserve many people alive. So therefore, do not be afraid; I will provide for you and your little ones." So he comforted them and spoke kindly to them. (NASB)

15. **The Lord brings grief at times, but he also shows mercy.**

Lamentations 3:31–33 For no one is abandoned by the Lord forever. Though he brings grief, he also shows compassion because of the greatness of his unfailing love. For he does not enjoy hurting people or causing them sorrow. (NLT)

16. **God decrees and brings both hardship and good times.**

Lamentations 3:37–42 Who can command things to happen without the Lord's permission? Does not the Most High send both calamity and good? Then why should we, mere humans, complain when we are punished for our sins? Instead, let us test and examine our ways. Let us turn back to the LORD. Let us lift our hearts and hands to God in heaven and say, "We have sinned and rebelled, and you have not forgiven us." (NLT)

17. **God faithfully cares for us as a shepherd cares for his sheep.**

Psalm 23

18. **When we please the Lord, he makes even our enemies to be at peace with us.**

Proverbs 16:7 When the LORD takes pleasure in anyone's way, he causes their enemies to make peace with them. (NIV)

19. **All rulers are under God's control.**

Proverbs 21:1 In the LORD's hand the king's heart is a stream of water that he channels toward all who please him. (NIV)

20. **God has sovereignly planned what shall come to pass and he sovereignly carries out his plans.**

Isaiah 46:10–13

Isaiah 46:10 I make known the end from the beginning, from ancient times, what is still to come. I say, "My purpose will stand, and I will do all that I please." (NIV)

**21. It is God who gives rain. Pray for rain in time of need.**

Zechariah 10:1 Ask the LORD for rain in the springtime; it is the LORD who sends the thunderstorms. He gives showers of rain to all people, and plants of the field to everyone. (NIV)

**22. The story of Jonah strikingly reveals God's providence.**

Jonah 1:4 But the LORD hurled a great wind upon the sea, and there was a mighty tempest on the sea, so that the ship threatened to break up.

Jonah 1:17 And the LORD appointed a great fish to swallow up Jonah. And Jonah was in the belly of the fish three days and three nights.

Jonah 2:10 And the LORD spoke to the fish, and it vomited Jonah out upon the dry land.

Jonah 4:6–8 Now the LORD God appointed a plant and made it come up over Jonah, that it might be a shade over his head, to save him from his discomfort. So Jonah was exceedingly glad because of the plant. But when dawn came up the next day, God appointed a worm that attacked the plant, so that it withered. When the sun rose, God appointed a scorching east wind, and the sun beat down on the head of Jonah so that he was faint. And he asked that he might die and said, "It is better for me to die than to live."

**23. God chose Jeremiah to be a prophet even before he was born.**

Jeremiah 1:4–6 Then the word of the LORD came to me, saying: "Before I formed you in the womb I knew you; before you were born I sanctified you; I ordained you a prophet to the nations." Then said I: "Ah, Lord God! Behold, I cannot speak, for I am a youth." (NKJV)

24. **God sovereignly works out his plans, his perfect will. No one can hinder or stop him.**

Proverbs 16:4 The LORD works out everything to its proper end—even the wicked for a day of disaster. (NIV)

Proverbs 16:9 In their hearts humans plan their course, but the LORD establishes their steps. (NIV)

Proverbs 16:33 The lot is cast into the lap, but its every decision is from the LORD. (NIV)

Proverbs 21:30 There is no wisdom, no insight, no plan that can succeed against the LORD. (NIV)

Psalm 135:6 The LORD does whatever pleases him, in the heavens and on the earth, in the seas and all their depths. (NIV)

25. **God sovereignly used Paul's imprisonment in Rome to advance the gospel.**

Philippians 1:12–14 Now I want you to know, brethren, that my circumstances have turned out for the greater progress of the gospel, so that my imprisonment in the cause of Christ has become well known throughout the whole praetorian guard and to everyone else, and that most of the brethren, trusting in the Lord because of my imprisonment, have far more courage to speak the word of God without fear. (NASB)

26. **God prepared Joseph to become governor over Egypt. Such acts of God reveal his personal involvement in the lives of his children.**

Acts 7:9–10 These patriarchs were jealous of their brother Joseph, and they sold him to be a slave in Egypt. But God was with him and rescued him from all his troubles. And God gave him favor before Pharaoh, king of Egypt. God also gave Joseph unusual wisdom, so that Pharaoh appointed him governor over all of Egypt and put him in charge of the palace. (NLT)

27. **God kept Moses alive and ordained that he should be educated in all the wisdom of Egypt so that he could lead the children of Israel.**

Acts 7:20–22 At that time Moses was born—a beautiful child in God's eyes. His parents cared for him at home for three months.

When they had to abandon him, Pharaoh's daughter adopted him and raised him as her own son. Moses was taught all the wisdom of the Egyptians, and he was powerful in both speech and action. (NLT)

28. God gave Daniel and his three friends special intellectual ability and wisdom to fulfill his purposes. See how God works for his children.

Daniel 1:17 As for these four youths, God gave them knowledge and intelligence in every branch of literature and wisdom; Daniel even understood all kinds of visions and dreams. (NASB)
Daniel 6:3–4 Then this Daniel began distinguishing himself among the commissioners and satraps because he possessed an extraordinary spirit, and the king planned to appoint him over the entire kingdom. (NASB)

29. God put it into the heart of the evil king Cyrus to allow his people to return to the promised land.

Ezra 1:1 Now in the first year of Cyrus king of Persia, in order to fulfill the word of the LORD by the mouth of Jeremiah, the LORD stirred up the spirit of Cyrus king of Persia, so that he sent a proclamation throughout all his kingdom, and also put it in writing. (NASB)

30. The hand of God was on Nehemiah; that's why King Artaxerxes granted his requests.

Nehemiah 2:4–9
Nehemiah 2:8 "And please give me a letter addressed to Asaph, the manager of the king's forest, instructing him to give me timber. I will need it to make beams for the gates of the Temple fortress, for the city walls, and for a house for myself." And the king granted these requests, because the gracious hand of God was on me. (NLT)

# Repentance

*See also* Progressive Sanctification, Overcoming Sin, Warnings

### 1. Jesus calls sinners to repentance.

Luke 5:27–32 *(The Pharisees objected that Jesus ate with tax collectors and sinners. Jesus explained exactly why he did this.)*
Luke 5:31–32 And Jesus answered them, "Those who are well have no need of a physician, but those who are sick. I have not come to call the righteous but sinners to repentance."

### 2. Jesus calls needy sinners to repentance that leads to salvation.

Matthew 4:17 From that time Jesus began to preach, saying, "Repent, for the kingdom of heaven is at hand."

### 3. Repentance must be from the heart, genuine.

Mark 7:20–23 He went on: "What comes out of a person is what defiles them. For it is from within, out of a person's heart, that evil thoughts come—sexual immorality, theft, murder, adultery, greed, malice, deceit, lewdness, envy, slander, arrogance and folly. All these evils come from inside and defile a person." (NIV)

Jeremiah 4:3–4 This is what the LORD says to the people of Judah and to Jerusalem: "Break up your unplowed ground and do not sow among thorns. Circumcise yourselves to the LORD, circumcise your hearts, you people of Judah and inhabitants of Jerusalem, or my wrath will flare up and burn like fire because of the evil you have done—burn with no one to quench it." (NIV)

Joel 2:12–13 "Even now," declares the LORD, "return to me with all your heart, with fasting and weeping and mourning." Rend your heart and not your garments. Return to the LORD your God, for he is gracious and compassionate, slow to anger and abounding in love, and he relents from sending calamity. (NIV)

4. **Godly sorrow brings repentance that leads to salvation.**

2 Corinthians 7:8–11 *(Motivated by love, Paul led the Corinthian Christians to a godly sorrow, which brought repentance and salvation.)*

2 Corinthians 7:10–11 For the kind of sorrow God wants us to experience leads us away from sin and results in salvation. There's no regret for that kind of sorrow. But worldly sorrow, which lacks repentance, results in spiritual death. Just see what this godly sorrow produced in you! Such earnestness, such concern to clear yourselves, such indignation, such alarm, such longing to see me, such zeal, and such a readiness to punish wrong. You showed that you have done everything necessary to make things right. (NLT)

5. **There is joy in heaven over one sinner who repents.**

Luke 15 *(Jesus taught this in the parables of the lost sheep, the lost coin, and the lost son.)*

Luke 15:7 Just so, I tell you, there will be more joy in heaven over one sinner who repents than over ninety-nine righteous persons who need no repentance.

6. **God calls sinners to seek him, to forsake their evil ways, and he promises to forgive them.**

Isaiah 55:6–7 Seek the LORD while he may be found; call upon him while he is near; let the wicked forsake his way, and the unrighteous man his thoughts; let him return to the LORD, that he may have compassion on him, and to our God, for he will abundantly pardon.

7. **God calls to repentance those who have set up idols in their hearts and practice evil.**

Ezekiel 14:1–11

Ezekiel 14:6 Therefore say to the house of Israel, Thus says the Lord GOD: Repent and turn away from your idols, and turn away your faces from all your abominations.

8. **When a wayward sinner repents and turns back to God, he will live.**

   **Ezekiel 18:21–22** But if a wicked person turns away from all his sins that he has committed and keeps all my statutes and does what is just and right, he shall surely live; he shall not die. None of the transgressions that he has committed shall be remembered against him; for the righteousness that he has done he shall live.

9. **God takes no pleasure in the death of the wicked.**

   **Ezekiel 18:23** Have I any pleasure in the death of the wicked, declares the Lord GOD, and not rather that he should turn from his way and live?

10. **The Lord urgently calls sinners to turn from their evil ways.**

    **Ezekiel 18:30–32** Therefore I will judge you, O house of Israel, every one according to his ways, declares the Lord GOD. Repent and turn from all your transgressions, lest iniquity be your ruin. Cast away from you all the transgressions that you have committed, and make yourselves a new heart and a new spirit! Why will you die, O house of Israel? For I have no pleasure in the death of anyone, declares the Lord GOD; so turn, and live.

11. **Jesus pronounced his judgment on those who refused to repent.**

    **Matthew 11:20–24** Then He began to denounce the cities in which most of His miracles were done, because they did not repent. "Woe to you, Chorazin! Woe to you, Bethsaida! For if the miracles had occurred in Tyre and Sidon which occurred in you, they would have repented long ago in sackcloth and ashes. Nevertheless I say to you, it will be more tolerable for Tyre and Sidon in the day of judgment than for you. And you, Capernaum, will not be exalted to heaven, will you? You will descend to Hades; for if the miracles had occurred in Sodom which occurred in you, it would have remained to this day. Nevertheless I say to you that it will be more tolerable for the land of Sodom in the day of judgment, than for you." (NASB)

12. Out of his kindness, God keeps calling sinners to repentance.

Romans 2:4 Or do you think lightly of the riches of His kindness and tolerance and patience, not knowing that the kindness of God leads you to repentance? (NASB)

13. If you stubbornly refuse to repent, God will punish you. If you do repent, he will forgive you and grant you eternal life.

Romans 2:5–11

Romans 2:5–6 But because of your stubbornness and unrepentant heart you are storing up wrath for yourself in the day of wrath and revelation of the righteous judgment of God, who will render to each person according to his deeds. (NASB)

14. Calamity comes to those who do not give heed to God's call to repentance.

Proverbs 1:24–33

Proverbs 1:24–28 Because I have called and you refused, I have stretched out my hand and no one regarded, because you disdained all my counsel, and would have none of my rebuke, I also will laugh at your calamity; I will mock when your terror comes, when your terror comes like a storm, and your destruction comes like a whirlwind, when distress and anguish come upon you. Then they will call on me, but I will not answer; they will seek me diligently, but they will not find me. (NKJV)

15. An adulterous woman repented and turned to Christ and was forgiven.

Luke 7:36–50

Luke 7:37–38 And behold, a woman in the city who was a sinner, when she knew that Jesus sat at the table in the Pharisee's house, brought an alabaster flask of fragrant oil, and stood at His feet behind Him weeping; and she began to wash His feet with her tears, and wiped them with the hair of her head; and she kissed His feet and anointed them with the fragrant oil. (NKJV)

Luke 7:48–50 Then He said to her, "Your sins are forgiven." And those who sat at the table with Him began to say to themselves,

"Who is this who even forgives sins?" Then He said to the woman, "Your faith has saved you. Go in peace." (NKJV)

16. **God poured out his anger on unrepentant Israelites.**

Isaiah 42:23–25 Who among you will give ear to this? Who will listen and hear for the time to come? Who gave Jacob for plunder, and Israel to the robbers? Was it not the Lord, He against whom we have sinned? For they would not walk in His ways, nor were they obedient to His law. Therefore He has poured on him the fury of His anger and the strength of battle; it has set him on fire all around, yet he did not know; and it burned him, yet he did not take it to heart. (NKJV)

17. **Return to the Lord and he will return to you.**

Malachi 3:7 "Return to me, and I will return to you," says the Lord Almighty. (NIV)

18. **Those who mourn on account of their sin are blessed.**

Matthew 5:4 Blessed are those who mourn, for they will be comforted. (NIV)

19. **If God's people turn from their wicked ways, he will forgive them.**

2 Chronicles 7:14 If my people who are called by my name humble themselves, and pray and seek my face and turn from their wicked ways, then I will hear from heaven and will forgive their sin and heal their land.

20. **Paul preached that all sinners must repent, turn to God, and prove their repentance by their deeds.**

Acts 26:19–20 Therefore, O King Agrippa, I was not disobedient to the heavenly vision, but declared first to those in Damascus, then in Jerusalem and throughout all the region of Judea, and also to the Gentiles, that they should repent and turn to God, performing deeds in keeping with their repentance.

# Salvation

## *(Leading a Person to Christ)*

### Apart from Christ, we are helpless and sinful.

*We are all sinners.*

1. **We are all born in sin.**

   **Psalm 51:5** Surely I was sinful at birth, sinful from the time my mother conceived me. (NIV)

2. **We all, like sheep, have gone astray.**

   **Isaiah 53:6** We all, like sheep, have gone astray, each of us has turned to our own way; and the LORD has laid on him the iniquity of us all. (NIV)

3. **All have sinned through Adam.**

   **Romans 5:12** Therefore, just as sin came into the world through one man, and death through sin, and so death spread to all men because all sinned.

   **Romans 5:19** For as by the one man's disobedience the many were made sinners, so by the one man's obedience the many will be made righteous.

4. **Jews and Gentiles alike are sinners.**

   **Romans 3:9–12** What then? Are we Jews any better off? No, not at all. For we have already charged that all, both Jews and Greeks, are under sin, as it is written: "None is righteous, no, not one; no one understands; no one seeks for God. All have turned aside; together they have become worthless; no one does good, not even one." **Romans 3:22–23** For there is no distinction: for all have sinned and fall short of the glory of God.

5. **We are like lost sheep whom Jesus goes out to seek.**

   Luke 15:3–7

6. **We are like the prodigal son.**

   Luke 15:11–24

7. **Even our righteous acts are as filthy rags.**

   **Isaiah 64:6** All of us have become like one who is unclean, and all our righteous acts are like filthy rags; we all shrivel up like a leaf, and like the wind our sins sweep us away. (NIV)

8. **If you claim to be without sin, you deceive yourself and even make God out to be a liar.**

   **1 John 1:8–10** If we say that we have no sin, we are deceiving ourselves and the truth is not in us. If we confess our sins, He is faithful and righteous to forgive us our sins and to cleanse us from all unrighteousness. If we say that we have not sinned, we make Him a liar and His word is not in us. (NASB)

9. **Apart from God's grace, our hearts are deceitful, beyond cure.**

   **Jeremiah 17:9** The heart is deceitful above all things, and desperately wicked; who can know it? (NKJV)

10. **In the light of God's holiness we see that we are very sinful. That is what happened to Isaiah.**

    **Isaiah 6:1–5** In the year that King Uzziah died, I saw the Lord sitting on a throne, high and lifted up, and the train of His robe filled the temple. Above it stood seraphim; each one had six wings: with two he covered his face, with two he covered his feet, and with two he flew. And one cried to another and said: "Holy, holy, holy is the LORD of hosts; the whole earth is full of His glory!" And the posts of the door were shaken by the voice of him who cried out, and the house was filled with smoke. So I said: "Woe is me, for I am undone! Because I am a man of unclean lips, and I dwell in the midst of a people of unclean lips; for my eyes have seen the King, the LORD of hosts." (NKJV)

## We are in spiritual bondage.

### 1. By nature all are in sin's bondage. Christ sets us free.

John 8:31–36

John 8:34–36 Jesus answered them, "Most assuredly, I say to you, whoever commits sin is a slave of sin. And a slave does not abide in the house forever, but a son abides forever. Therefore if the Son makes you free, you shall be free indeed." (NKJV)

### 2. To continue to live in sin is bondage.

2 Peter 2:19 They [false prophets] promise . . . freedom, while they themselves are slaves of depravity—for "people are slaves to whatever has mastered them." (NIV)

### 3. Jesus sets us free.

Romans 6:16–18 Don't you know that when you offer your-selves to someone as obedient slaves, you are slaves of the one you obey—whether you are slaves to sin, which leads to death, or to obedience, which leads to righteousness? But thanks be to God that, though you used to be slaves to sin, you have come to obey from your heart the pattern of teaching that has now claimed your allegiance. You have been set free from sin and have become slaves to righteousness. (NIV)

## We are alienated from God.

### 1. Outside of Christ we are at odds with God.

Colossians 1:21–22 And you, who once were alienated and hostile in mind, doing evil deeds, he has now reconciled in his body of flesh by his death, in order to present you holy and blameless and above reproach before him.

2. **Without Christ we are without hope.**

Ephesians 2:12–13 Remember that you were at that time separated from Christ, alienated from the commonwealth of Israel and strangers to the covenants of promise, having no hope and without God in the world. But now in Christ Jesus you who once were far off have been brought near by the blood of Christ.

## Knowledge of sin comes by the law of God.

1. **Through knowledge of the law we become conscious of sin.**

Romans 3:20 For by works of the law no human being will be justified in his sight, since through the law comes knowledge of sin.

2. **The law helps us understand sin.**

Romans 7:7 What then shall we say? That the law is sin? By no means! Yet if it had not been for the law, I would not have known sin. I would not have known what it is to covet if the law had not said, "You shall not covet."

3. **Jesus gave us his summary of the law.**

Matthew 22:37–40 And he said to him, "You shall love the Lord your God with all your heart and with all your soul and with all your mind. This is the great and first commandment. And a second is like it: You shall love your neighbor as yourself. On these two commandments depend all the Law and the Prophets."

4. **God has given us the Ten Commandments.**

Exodus 20:1–17

*God in his justice punishes sinners.*

1. God first revealed his justice to Adam.

   Genesis 2:16–17 And the LORD God commanded the man, saying, "You may surely eat of every tree of the garden, but of the tree of the knowledge of good and evil you shall not eat, for in the day that you eat of it you shall surely die."

2. The result of sin is death.

   Romans 5:12 Therefore, just as sin came into the world through one man, and death through sin, and so death spread to all men because all sinned.

   Romans 6:23 For the wages of sin is death, but the free gift of God is eternal life in Christ Jesus our Lord.

3. By nature we are all under the curse of God.

   Galatians 3:10 For all who rely on works of the law are under a curse; for it is written, "Cursed be everyone who does not abide by all things written in the Book of the Law, and do them."
   See also Warnings.

*We cannot save ourselves in any way.*

1. By nature we are at enmity with God.

   Romans 8:7–8 For the mind that is set on the flesh is hostile to God, for it does not submit to God's law; indeed, it cannot. Those who are in the flesh cannot please God.

2. By nature we are dead in sin and are objects of God's wrath.

   Ephesians 2:1–5 And you were dead in your trespasses and sins, in which you formerly walked according to the course of this world, according to the prince of the power of the air, of the spirit that is now working in the sons of disobedience. Among them we too all formerly lived in the lusts of our flesh, indulging the desires of the flesh and of the mind, and were by nature children of wrath, even as the rest. But God, being rich in mercy, because of His great love with which He loved us, even when we were dead in our transgressions, made us alive together with Christ (by grace you have been saved). (NASB)

3. We are saved only by grace, through faith.

Ephesians 2:8–9 For by grace you have been saved through faith; and that not of yourselves, it is the gift of God; not as a result of works, so that no one may boast. (NASB)

4. God saves us through a rebirth and renewal by the Holy Spirit.

Titus 3:4–7 But when the kindness of God our Savior and His love for mankind appeared, He saved us, not on the basis of deeds which we have done in righteousness, but according to His mercy, by the washing of regeneration and renewing by the Holy Spirit, whom He poured out upon us richly through Jesus Christ our Savior, so that being justified by His grace we would be made heirs according to the hope of eternal life. (NASB)

## Jesus saves us by grace, through faith.

*Jesus suffered and died for sinners; those who believe in him will be saved.*

1. Isaiah depicts the suffering servant of Jehovah.

Isaiah 53:1–11
Isaiah 53:4–6 Surely He has borne our griefs and carried our sorrows; yet we esteemed Him stricken, smitten by God, and afflicted. But He was wounded for our transgressions, He was bruised for our iniquities; the chastisement for our peace was upon Him, and by His stripes we are healed. All we like sheep have gone astray; we have turned, every one, to his own way; and the LORD has laid on Him the iniquity of us all. (NKJV)

2. All who receive Christ by faith are saved.

John 1:12 To all who did receive him, to those who believed in his name, he gave the right to become children of God. (NIV)

3. As was prophesied, God gave his only Son so that those who believe in him may have eternal life.

John 3:14–16 "Just as Moses lifted up the snake in the wilderness, so the Son of Man must be lifted up, that everyone who believes may have eternal life in him." For God so loved the world that he gave his one and only Son, that whoever believes in him shall not perish but have eternal life. (NIV)

4. Jesus died for his sheep.

John 10:11, 14–15 "I am the good shepherd. The good shepherd lays down his life for the sheep. . . . I am the good shepherd; I know my sheep and my sheep know me—just as the Father knows me and I know the Father—and I lay down my life for the sheep." (NIV)

5. His sheep hear Jesus' voice and follow him and receive eternal life.

John 10:27–28 My sheep listen to my voice; I know them, and they follow me. I give them eternal life, and they shall never perish; no one will snatch them out of my hand. (NIV)

6. We are redeemed through the blood of Christ.

1 Peter 1:18–19 For you know that God paid a ransom to save you from the empty life you inherited from your ancestors. And the ransom he paid was not mere gold or silver. It was the precious blood of Christ, the sinless, spotless Lamb of God. (NLT)

7. Christ loved the church and gave himself for her.

Ephesians 5:25–27 For husbands, this means love your wives, just as Christ loved the church. He gave up his life for her to make her holy and clean, washed by the cleansing of God's word. He did this to present her to himself as a glorious church without a spot or wrinkle or any other blemish. Instead, she will be holy and without fault. (NLT)

8. Jesus is the only mediator.

1 Timothy 2:5–6 For there is only one God and one Mediator who can reconcile God and humanity—the man Christ Jesus. He gave his life to purchase freedom for everyone. This is the message God gave to the world at just the right time. (NLT)

9. Christ died for undeserving sinners, for many gracious purposes.

Romans 5:8 But God demonstrates His own love toward us, in that while we were yet sinners, Christ died for us. (NASB)

Philippians 2:8 Being found in appearance as a man, He humbled Himself by becoming obedient to the point of death, even death on a cross. (NASB)

2 Corinthians 5:21 He made Him who knew no sin to be sin on our behalf, so that we might become the righteousness of God in Him. (NASB)

John 1:29 The next day he saw Jesus coming to him and said, "Behold, the Lamb of God who takes away the sin of the world!" (NASB)

1 John 4:9–10 By this the love of God was manifested in us, that God has sent His only begotten Son into the world so that we might live through Him. In this is love, not that we loved God, but that He loved us and sent His Son to be the propitiation for our sins. (NASB)

Galatians 3:13 Christ redeemed us from the curse of the law by becoming a curse for us—for it is written, "Cursed is everyone who is hanged on a tree."

1 Peter 2:24 He himself bore our sins in his body on the tree, that we might die to sin and live to righteousness. By his wounds you have been healed.

1 Peter 3:18 For Christ also suffered once for sins, the righteous for the unrighteous, that he might bring us to God, being put to death in the flesh but made alive in the spirit.

Hebrews 9:14–15 Just think how much more the blood of Christ will purify our consciences from sinful deeds so that we can worship the living God. For by the power of the eternal Spirit, Christ offered himself to God as a perfect sacrifice for our sins. (NLT)

10. **We are forgiven, justified, and cleared of all guilt and condemnation by faith in Jesus Christ.**

    **Romans 3:21–24** But now the righteousness of God apart from the law is revealed, being witnessed by the Law and the Prophets, even the righteousness of God, through faith in Jesus Christ, to all and on all who believe. For there is no difference; for all have sinned and fall short of the glory of God, being justified freely by His grace through the redemption that is in Christ Jesus. (NKJV)

    **Romans 5:1** Therefore, having been justified by faith, we have peace with God through our Lord Jesus Christ. (NKJV)

    **Romans 8:1** Therefore there is now no condemnation for those who are in Christ Jesus. (NASB)

    **Romans 10:9–13** If you confess with your mouth the Lord Jesus and believe in your heart that God has raised Him from the dead, you will be saved. For with the heart one believes unto righteousness, and with the mouth confession is made unto salvation. For the Scripture says, "Whoever believes on Him will not be put to shame." For there is no distinction between Jew and Greek, for the same Lord over all is rich to all who call upon Him. For whoever calls on the name of the Lord shall be saved. (NKJV)

    See also Forgiveness of Sins.

*Examples of those saved by grace, through faith.*

1. Levi, the tax collector.

    Luke 5:27–32

2. Zacchaeus, the tax collector.

    **Luke 19:9–10** Jesus said to him, "Today salvation has come to this house, because this man, too, is a son of Abraham. For the Son of Man came to seek and to save the lost." (NIV)

3. The penitent woman who wept at Jesus' feet.

> Luke 7:48, 50 Then Jesus said to her, "Your sins are forgiven. . . . Your faith has saved you; go in peace." (NIV)

4. Many notorious sinners represented in Jesus' parables.

> Luke 15:1–2 Now the tax collectors and sinners were all gathering around to hear Jesus. But the Pharisees and the teachers of the law muttered, "This man welcomes sinners and eats with them." (NIV)
> Luke 15:3–7 *(the parable of the lost sheep)*
> Luke 15:8–10 *(the parable of the lost coin)*
> Luke 15:11–31 *(the parable of the prodigal son)*

5. The Samaritan woman at Jacob's well.

> John 4:1–26

6. The murderer on the cross.

> Luke 23:39–43
> Luke 23:43 Jesus answered him, "Truly I tell you, today you will be with me in paradise." (NIV)

7. Saul, the persecutor of the church, who became Paul, the great missionary.

> Acts 9:1–19 *(Paul's conversion)*
> 1 Timothy 1:13–16 Even though I was formerly a blasphemer and a persecutor and a violent aggressor. Yet I was shown mercy because I acted ignorantly in unbelief; and the grace of our Lord was more than abundant, with the faith and love which are found in Christ Jesus. It is a trustworthy statement, deserving full acceptance, that Christ Jesus came into the world to save sinners, among whom I am foremost of all. Yet for this reason I found mercy, so that in me as the foremost, Jesus Christ might demonstrate His perfect patience as an example for those who would believe in Him for eternal life. (NASB)

8. The Philippian jailer.

Acts 16:25–26

Acts 16:30–31 Then he brought them out and asked, "Sirs, what must I do to be saved?" They replied, "Believe in the Lord Jesus and you will be saved, along with everyone in your household." (NLT)

## The Lord calls sinners like you and me.

1. **God calls those who are spiritually hungry and thirsty.**

Isaiah 55:1–3 Is anyone thirsty? Come and drink—even if you have no money! Come, take your choice of wine or milk—it's all free! Why spend your money on food that does not give you strength? Why pay for food that does you no good? Listen to me, and you will eat what is good. You will enjoy the finest food. Come to me with your ears wide open. Listen, and you will find life. I will make an everlasting covenant with you. I will give you all the unfailing love I promised to David. (NLT)

2. **Jesus is the bread of life and the living water, and he calls sinners to come to him.**

John 6:35 Jesus replied, "I am the bread of life. Whoever comes to me will never be hungry again. Whoever believes in me will never be thirsty." (NLT)

John 7:37–38 On the last day, the climax of the festival, Jesus stood and shouted to the crowds, "Anyone who is thirsty may come to me! Anyone who believes in me may come and drink! For the Scriptures declare, 'Rivers of living water will flow from his heart.'" (NLT)

Revelation 22:17–18 The Spirit and the bride say, "Come." Let anyone who hears this say, "Come." Let anyone who is thirsty come. Let anyone who desires drink freely from the water of life. (NLT)

3. Jesus calls those who are weary and burdened.

Matthew 11:28–30 Come to Me, all you who labor and are heavy laden, and I will give you rest. Take My yoke upon you and learn from Me, for I am gentle and lowly in heart, and you will find rest for your souls. For My yoke is easy and My burden is light. (NKJV)

4. He calls us to enter through the narrow gate.

Matthew 7:13–14 Enter by the narrow gate; for wide is the gate and broad is the way that leads to destruction, and there are many who go in by it. Because narrow is the gate and difficult is the way which leads to life, and there are few who find it. (NKJV)

5. He calls us to repent and believe the gospel.

Mark 1:14–15 Now after John was put in prison, Jesus came to Galilee, preaching the gospel of the kingdom of God, and saying, "The time is fulfilled, and the kingdom of God is at hand. Repent, and believe in the gospel." (NKJV)

6. Seek the Lord while he may be found.

Isaiah 55:6–7 Seek the Lord while you can find him. Call on him now while he is near. Let the wicked change their ways and banish the very thought of doing wrong. Let them turn to the Lord that he may have mercy on them. Yes, turn to our God, for he will forgive generously. (NLT)

7. Today, if you hear his voice, don't harden your heart.

Hebrews 3:7–19
Hebrews 3:7–9 So, as the Holy Spirit says: "Today, if you hear his voice, do not harden your hearts as you did in the rebellion, during the time of testing in the wilderness, where your ancestors tested and tried me, though for forty years they saw what I did." (NIV)

8. The Lord will never turn a sinner away.

John 6:37 All those the Father gives me will come to me, and whoever comes to me I will never drive away. (NIV)

Romans 10:13 Everyone who calls on the name of the Lord will be saved. (NIV)

## We are saved to joyfully obey and serve the Lord.

1. Offer yourself as a living sacrifice unto God.

Romans 12:1–2 And so, dear brothers and sisters, I plead with you to give your bodies to God because of all he has done for you. Let them be a living and holy sacrifice—the kind he will find acceptable. This is truly the way to worship him. Don't copy the behavior and customs of this world, but let God transform you into a new person by changing the way you think. Then you will learn to know God's will for you, which is good and pleasing and perfect. (NLT)

2. We are saved to bear much fruit, through Jesus Christ, the vine.

John 15:1–8

John 15:8 This is to my Father's glory, that you bear much fruit, showing yourselves to be my disciples. (NIV)

3. We are saved to be dead to sin, alive to God, and slaves to righteousness.

Romans 6:1–23

4. We are called to live a new life through the power of the Holy Spirit.

Romans 8:1–14
Ephesians 5:1–21

5. The Holy Spirit helps us to bear fruit.

Galatians 5:13–26

6. Christ died for us so that we should no longer live for ourselves but for him.

   2 Corinthians 5:15 And he died for all, that those who live should no longer live for themselves but for him who died for them and was raised again. (NIV)

   For more Scriptures on living the life of gratitude for our salvation see Loving God, Loving and Serving Others, Obedience, Progressive Sanctification.

# Self-Centeredness

*See also* Loving and Serving Others (as the opposite of self-centeredness)

1. **Love is not self-seeking.**

   **1 Corinthians 13:5** [Love] does not dishonor others, it is not self-seeking, it is not easily angered, it keeps no record of wrongs. (NIV)

2. **Selfish ambition brings its bitter fruit.**

   **James 3:14–16** But if you are bitterly jealous and there is selfish ambition in your heart, don't cover up the truth with boasting and lying. For jealousy and selfishness are not God's kind of wisdom. Such things are earthly, unspiritual, and demonic. For wherever there is jealousy and selfish ambition, there you will find disorder and evil of every kind. (NLT)

3. **Jesus condemned James and John for their self-seeking attitude, and he calls us all to humble service.**

   Matthew 20:20–28
   **Matthew 20:26–28** But among you it will be different. Whoever wants to be a leader among you must be your servant, and whoever wants to be first among you must become your slave. For even the Son of Man came not to be served but to serve others and to give his life as a ransom for many. (NLT)

4. **Jesus calls us to self-denial.**

   **Luke 9:23–25** And he said to all, "If anyone would come after me, let him deny himself and take up his cross daily and follow me. For whoever would save his life will lose it, but whoever loses his life for my sake will save it. For what does it profit a man if he gains the whole world and loses or forfeits himself?"

5. **Don't be self-centered, but think of others.**

1 Corinthians 10:24 Let no one seek his own good, but the good of his neighbor.

6. **Follow Jesus' example by thinking of how to please others.**

Luke 9:23–25 And he said to all, "If anyone would come after me, let him deny himself and take up his cross daily and follow me. For whoever would save his life will lose it, but whoever loses his life for my sake will save it. For what does it profit a man if he gains the whole world and loses or forfeits himself?"

Romans 15:2–3 Let each of us please his neighbor for his good, to build him up. For Christ did not please himself.

7. **Do not just think of yourself. Be like Jesus; think also of others. Be self-giving.**

Philippians 2:3–8
Philippians 2:3–5 Don't be selfish; don't try to impress others. Be humble, thinking of others as better than yourselves. Don't look out only for your own interests, but take an interest in others, too. You must have the same attitude that Christ Jesus had. (NLT)

# Self-Control, Self-Discipline

1. Lack of self-control brings misery.

   Proverbs 25:28 A man without self-control is like a city broken into and left without walls.

2. One who gives full vent to his anger acts like a fool; one who keeps himself under control is wise.

   Proverbs 29:11 A fool gives full vent to his spirit, but a wise man quietly holds it back.

3. Every Christian can be self-controlled; it's a fruit of the Spirit.

   Galatians 5:22–23 But the fruit of the Spirit is . . . gentleness, self-control.

4. Self-discipline is a gift of God.

   2 Timothy 1:7 For God gave us a spirit not of fear but of power and love and self-control.

5. We are commanded to be self-controlled.

   1 Peter 1:13 Think clearly and exercise self-control. (NLT)

6. One can and must develop self-control—put a lot of effort into it.

   2 Peter 1:5–6 For this very reason, make every effort to supplement your faith with virtue, and virtue with knowledge, and knowledge with self-control, and self-control with steadfastness, and steadfastness with godliness.

7. **Both old and young alike must learn self-control.**

**Titus 2:2–6** Older men are to be sober-minded, dignified, self-controlled, sound in faith, in love, and in steadfastness. Older women likewise are to be reverent in behavior, not slanderers or slaves to much wine. They are to teach what is good, and so train the young women to love their husbands and children, to be self-controlled, pure, working at home, kind, and submissive to their own husbands, that the word of God may not be reviled. Likewise, urge the younger men to be self-controlled.

8. **There is a time for everything. To be self-controlled is to do everything in its time.**

**Ecclesiastes 3:1–8**

9. **We can control our thinking.**

**2 Corinthians 10:5** We destroy arguments and every lofty opinion raised against the knowledge of God, and take every thought captive to obey Christ.

10. **Exercising self-control is walking in the light.**

**1 Thessalonians 5:4–8** But you are not in darkness, brothers, for that day to surprise you like a thief. For you are all children of light, children of the day. We are not of the night or of the darkness. So then let us not sleep, as others do, but let us keep awake and be sober. For those who sleep, sleep at night, and those who get drunk, are drunk at night. But since we belong to the day, let us be sober, having put on the breastplate of faith and love, and for a helmet the hope of salvation.

11. **Be self-controlled in your talking; control your tongue.**

**Proverbs 20:19** A gossip goes around telling secrets, so don't hang around with chatterers. (NLT)
See also Communication for more on exercising self-control in talking.

12. **Exercise self-control and say no to all ungodliness.**

**Titus 2:11–12** For the grace of God has appeared, bringing salvation for all people, training us to renounce ungodliness and worldly passions, and to live self-controlled, upright, and godly lives in the present age.

13. **Be motivated by Christ's redeeming love.**

**Titus 2:13–14** . . . while we wait for the blessed hope—the appearing of the glory of our great God and Savior, Jesus Christ, who gave himself for us to redeem us from all wickedness and to purify for himself a people that are his very own, eager to do what is good. (NIV)

14. **Be neither wishy-washy, nor easily moved by others.**

**1 Corinthians 15:58** My dear brothers and sisters, stand firm. Let nothing move you. Always give yourselves fully to the work of the Lord, because you know that your labor in the Lord is not in vain. (NIV)

# Self-Pity, Brooding

1. Elijah yielded to self-pity for a time and fled to Horeb.

   **1 Kings 19**
   **1 Kings 19:4–5** Then he went on alone into the wilderness, traveling all day. He sat down under a solitary broom tree and prayed that he might die. "I have had enough, LORD," he said. "Take my life, for I am no better than my ancestors who have already died." Then he lay down and slept under the broom tree. (NLT)

2. God confronted Elijah.

   **1 Kings 19:9** And behold, the word of the LORD came to him, and he said to him, "What are you doing here, Elijah?"

3. Listen to Elijah's self-pity.

   **1 Kings 19:10** He said, "I have been very jealous for the LORD, the God of hosts. For the people of Israel have forsaken your covenant, thrown down your altars, and killed your prophets with the sword, and I, even I only, am left, and they seek my life, to take it away."

4. God dealt with Elijah's problem.

   **1 Kings 19:11–18**

5. Asaph, the psalmist, also fell into the sin of self-pity for a time.

   **Psalm 73**

6. **Listen to Asaph's self-pity.**

Psalm 73:13–14 All in vain have I kept my heart clean and washed my hands in innocence. For all the day long I have been stricken and rebuked every morning.

7. **Asaph recovered from his self-pity.**

Psalm 73:15–28

8. **The Lord directs us to a cure for self-pity.**

Psalm 37

9. **Turn from self-pity.**

Proverbs 15:13 A glad heart makes a cheerful face, but by sorrow of heart the spirit is crushed.

10. **Jonah became angry and was filled with self-pity, for which God rebuked him.**

Jonah 4:1–4
Jonah 4:3–4 "Therefore now, O Lord, please take my life from me, for it is better for me to die than to live." And the Lord said, "Do you do well to be angry?"

# Sex Life

*See also* Song of Songs

### 1. Sex is God-given.

Hebrews 13:4 Let marriage be held in honor among all, and let the marriage bed be undefiled, for God will judge the sexually immoral and adulterous.

### 2. Fulfill your duty to your spouse.

1 Corinthians 7:3 The husband should fulfill his wife's sexual needs, and the wife should fulfill her husband's needs. (NLT)

### 3. Your body also belongs to your spouse.

1 Corinthians 7:4 The wife gives authority over her body to her husband, and the husband gives authority over his body to his wife. (NLT)

### 4. Refrain only by mutual consent; for refraining can lead to temptation.

1 Corinthians 7:5 Do not deprive each other of sexual relations, unless you both agree to refrain from sexual intimacy for a limited time so you can give yourselves more completely to prayer. Afterward, you should come together again so that Satan won't be able to tempt you because of your lack of self-control. (NLT)

### 5. Find satisfaction in your spouse.

Proverbs 5:18–20 Let your fountain be blessed, and rejoice in the wife of your youth, a lovely deer, a graceful doe. Let her breasts fill you at all times with delight; be intoxicated always in her love. Why should you be intoxicated, my son, with a forbidden woman and embrace the bosom of an adulteress?

# Sexual Immorality

*See also* **Adultery, Homosexuality**

**1. Looking on a woman lustfully is adulterous.**

**Matthew 5:27–28** You have heard that it was said, "You shall not commit adultery." But I say to you that everyone who looks at a woman with lustful intent has already committed adultery with her in his heart.

**2. Spiritual surgery may be needed to avoid immorality.**

**Matthew 5:29–30** If your right eye causes you to sin, tear it out and throw it away. For it is better that you lose one of your members than that your whole body be thrown into hell. And if your right hand causes you to sin, cut it off and throw it away. For it is better that you lose one of your members than that your whole body go into hell.

**3. Put to death sexual immorality.**

**Colossians 3:5–7** Therefore consider the members of your earthly body as dead to immorality, impurity, passion, evil desire, and greed, which amounts to idolatry. For it is because of these things that the wrath of God will come upon the sons of disobedience, and in them you also once walked, when you were living in them. (NASB)

**4. You can overcome sins of sexual immorality.**

**Proverbs 4:23** Watch over your heart with all diligence, for from it flow the springs of life. (NASB)
**Proverbs 4:24–27** Put away from you a deceitful mouth and put devious speech far from you. Let your eyes look directly ahead and let your gaze be fixed straight in front of you. Watch the

path of your feet and all your ways will be established. Do not turn to the right nor to the left; turn your foot from evil. (NASB)

5. **Sexual sins come from the heart.**

   **Matthew 15:19** For out of the heart come evil thoughts, murder, adultery, sexual immorality.

6. **Sexual immorality, including premarital sex (fornication), is described in detail as sin against God and your body, the temple of the Holy Spirit.**

   **1 Corinthians 6:12–20**

7. **The sexually immoral will not inherit the kingdom of God.**

   **1 Corinthians 6:9–10** Do you not know that the unrighteous will not inherit the kingdom of God? Do not be deceived: neither the sexually immoral, nor idolaters, nor adulterers, nor men who practice homosexuality, nor thieves, nor the greedy, nor drunkards, nor revilers, nor swindlers will inherit the kingdom of God.

8. **God can cleanse you from the sin of sexual immorality.**

   **1 Corinthians 6:11** And such were some of you. But you were washed, you were sanctified, you were justified in the name of the Lord Jesus Christ and by the Spirit of our God.

9. **You can overcome sexual immorality through the Holy Spirit.**

   **Galatians 5:16–18** But I say, walk by the Spirit, and you will not gratify the desires of the flesh. For the desires of the flesh are against the Spirit, and the desires of the Spirit are against the flesh, for these are opposed to each other, to keep you from doing the things you want to do. But if you are led by the Spirit, you are not under the law.

10. **All immorality is forbidden. Walk as children of light. Be very careful how you live.**

    **Ephesians 5:3–17**

11. Jesus can set you free.

    John 8:31–36

12. Purify yourself out of reverence for God.

    2 Corinthians 7:1 Therefore, having these promises, beloved, let us cleanse ourselves from all defilement of flesh and spirit, perfecting holiness in the fear of God. (NASB)

13. Christians must no longer use parts of the body for sin; one can and must change.

    Romans 6:15–23

14. The destruction of Sodom and Gomorrah is a warning for all sexually immoral people.

    2 Peter 2:4–10
    Jude 6–7 And angels who did not keep their own domain, but abandoned their proper abode, He has kept in eternal bonds under darkness for the judgment of the great day, just as Sodom and Gomorrah and the cities around them, since they in the same way as these indulged in gross immorality and went after strange flesh, are exhibited as an example in undergoing the punishment of eternal fire. (NASB)

15. God wants all of us to avoid sexual immorality, including premarital sex, and to learn to control our own bodies.

    1 Thessalonians 4:3–6 For this is the will of God, your sanctification; that is, that you abstain from sexual immorality; that each of you know how to possess his own vessel in sanctification and honor, not in lustful passion, like the Gentiles who do not know God; and that no man transgress and defraud his brother in the matter because the Lord is the avenger in all these things, just as we also told you before and solemnly warned you. (NASB)

# Temptation

*See also* Overcoming Sin, Progressive Sanctification

1. **Satan subtly tempted Eve.**

    **Genesis 3:1–4** Now the serpent was more crafty than any of the wild animals the LORD God had made. He said to the woman, "Did God really say, 'You must not eat from any tree in the garden'?" The woman said to the serpent, "We may eat fruit from the trees in the garden, but God did say, 'You must not eat fruit from the tree that is in the middle of the garden, and you must not touch it, or you will die.'" "You will not certainly die," the serpent said to the woman. (NIV)

2. **The devil still prowls around like a lion, seeking whom he may devour.**

    **1 Peter 5:8–9** Be alert and of sober mind. Your enemy the devil prowls around like a roaring lion looking for someone to devour. Resist him, standing firm in the faith, because you know that the family of believers throughout the world is undergoing the same kind of sufferings. (NIV)

3. **Satan at times comes as an angel of light.**

    **2 Corinthians 11:14–15** No wonder, for even Satan disguises himself as an angel of light. Therefore it is not surprising if his servants also disguise themselves as servants of righteousness, whose end will be according to their deeds. (NASB)

4. **At times, Satan uses others to entice us.**

    **Proverbs 1:10** My son, if sinful men entice you, do not give in to them. (NIV)

215

5. God tempts no one. Each one is tempted when, by his own desire, he is dragged away and enticed.

James 1:13–15 Let no one say when he is tempted, "I am being tempted by God"; for God cannot be tempted by evil, and He Himself does not tempt anyone. But each one is tempted when he is carried away and enticed by his own lust. Then when lust has conceived, it gives birth to sin; and when sin is accomplished, it brings forth death. (NASB)

6. Resist the devil.

James 4:7 Submit therefore to God. Resist the devil and he will flee from you. (NASB)

7. Jesus was tempted by the devil.

Matthew 4:1–11

8. Jesus won by using the sword of the Spirit, God's Word, each time.

Matthew 4:4, 7, 10 *(Each time Jesus said, "It is written.")*

9. Jesus tells us to watch and pray, lest we should yield to temptation.

Matthew 6:13 And lead us not into temptation, but deliver us from the evil one. (NIV)

Matthew 26:41 Watch and pray so that you will not fall into temptation. The spirit is willing, but the flesh is weak. (NIV)

10. Every Christian should take heed, lest he or she should fall.

1 Corinthians 10:12 Therefore let him who thinks he stands take heed that he does not fall. (NASB)

11. Put on the whole armor of God to fight against the devil's schemes.

Ephesians 6:10–18

Ephesians 6:10–12 Finally, be strong in the Lord and in the strength of his might. Put on the whole armor of God, that you may be able to stand against the schemes of the devil. For we do not wrestle against flesh and blood, but against the rulers, against the authorities, against the cosmic powers over this present darkness, against the spiritual forces of evil in the heavenly places.

12. When he was tempted by Potiphar's wife to commit adultery, Joseph refused to sin against God.

Genesis 39:6–20

Genesis 39:9–10 "He is not greater in this house than I am, nor has he kept back anything from me except yourself, because you are his wife. How then can I do this great wickedness and sin against God?" And as she spoke to Joseph day after day, he would not listen to her, to lie beside her or to be with her.

# Training Children

*See also* **Youth**

1. God requires parents to rear their children in a God-centered way. The primary objective must be that your children know, believe in, love, reverence, and serve the Lord.

   **Deuteronomy 6:6–7** And these words that I command you today shall be on your heart. You shall teach them diligently to your children, and shall talk of them when you sit in your house, and when you walk by the way, and when you lie down, and when you rise.

   **John 17:3** And this is eternal life, that they know you the only true God, and Jesus Christ whom you have sent.

   **Ephesians 6:4** Fathers, do not provoke your children to anger, but bring them up in the discipline and instruction of the Lord.

2. The father is primarily responsible for child training.

   **Ephesians 6:4**

3. Like the psalmist David, all children are conceived and born in sin. Parents must seek to lead them to a saving knowledge of Jesus Christ.

   **Psalm 51:5** For I was born a sinner—yes, from the moment my mother conceived me. (NLT)

4. Parents must shepherd the child's heart, not only discipline, not merely attempting to correct outward behavior. When anyone sins it arises out of the heart.

   **Proverbs 4:23** Guard your heart above all else, for it determines the course of your life. (NLT)

Mark 7:21–23 For from within, out of a person's heart, come evil thoughts, sexual immorality, theft, murder, adultery, greed, wickedness, deceit, lustful desires, envy, slander, pride, and foolishness. All these vile things come from within; they are what defile you. (NLT)

5. Much of a child's sinful behavior arises out of a self-centered, selfish attitude.

See also Loving and Serving Others, Self-Centeredness.

6. Parents must give biblical instruction to their children, not just lay down rules and expectations.

Deuteronomy 6:6–7; Ephesians 6:4 *(See #1.)*

Proverbs 1:8–9 My son, hear the instruction of your father, and do not forsake the law of your mother; for they will be a graceful ornament on your head, and chains about your neck. (NKJV)

7. The Holy Spirit works through the Word of God to develop spiritual growth, biblical change in the lives of children and adults alike. Jesus prayed for this work of grace in his high priestly prayer.

John 17:17 Sanctify them by the truth; your word is truth. (NIV)

8. Your parental calling is similar to that which God gave to Abraham, the father of believers.

Genesis 18:19 For I have known him, in order that he may command his children and his household after him, that they keep the way of the LORD, to do righteousness and justice, that the LORD may bring to Abraham what He has spoken to him. (NKJV)

9. Parents must set a godly example for their children to learn by and to follow.

Deuteronomy 6:4–6 Hear, O Israel: The LORD our God, the LORD is one! You shall love the LORD your God with all your heart, with all your soul, and with all your strength. And these words which I command you today shall be in your heart. (NKJV)

10. **The father must manage his family well and see that his children obey him with proper respect.**

    **1 Timothy 3:4** He must manage his own family well, having children who respect and obey him. (NLT)

11. **Do not exasperate your children by unjust requirements or undue discipline.**

    **Ephesians 6:4** *(See #1.)*
    **Colossians 3:21** Fathers, do not aggravate your children, or they will become discouraged. (NLT)

12. **Love requires faithful discipline.**

    **Proverbs 13:24** Whoever spares the rod hates his son, but he who loves him is diligent to discipline him.
    **Proverbs 22:15** Folly is bound up in the heart of a child, but the rod of discipline drives it far from him.
    **Proverbs 23:13–14** Do not withhold discipline from a child; if you strike him with a rod, he will not die. If you strike him with the rod, you will save his soul from Sheol.
    **Proverbs 29:15** The rod and reproof give wisdom, but a child left to himself brings shame to his mother.
    **Proverbs 29:17** Discipline your son, and he will give you rest; he will give delight to your heart.

13. **Follow God's pattern, for he lovingly disciplines his children for their good.**

    **Hebrews 12:5–11**

14. **He is motivated by love for his children.**

    **Hebrews 12:6** For the Lord disciplines the one he loves, and chastises every son whom he receives.

15. God intends for discipline to be painful. He always does it for our good, that it may bear rich fruit in our lives.

    Hebrews 12:11 For the moment all discipline seems painful rather than pleasant, but later it yields the peaceful fruit of righteousness to those who have been trained by it.

16. The Lord condemned Eli for being an indulgent parent.

    1 Samuel 3:1–18
    1 Samuel 3:13 I have warned him that judgment is coming upon his family forever, because his sons are blaspheming God and he hasn't disciplined them. (NLT)

17. Train a child in the way he should go.

    Proverbs 22:6 Start children off on the way they should go, and even when they are old they will not turn from it. (NIV)

18. Unless the Lord builds the house . . .

    Psalm 127:1–2 Unless the LORD builds a house, the work of the builders is wasted. Unless the LORD protects a city, guarding it with sentries will do no good. It is useless for you to work so hard from early morning until late at night, anxiously working for food to eat; for God gives rest to his loved ones. (NLT)

19. Children are a heritage from the Lord.

    Psalm 127:3 Children are a gift from the LORD; they are a reward from him. (NLT)

# Trust, Faith in God

*See also* Comfort, Fear, Providence of God

### 1. Trust in the Lord.

Proverbs 3:5–6 Trust in the LORD with all your heart, and do not lean on your own understanding. In all your ways acknowledge him, and he will make straight your paths.

### 2. Nothing is too hard for God.

Jeremiah 32:17, 26–27 "Ah, Sovereign LORD, you have made the heavens and the earth by your great power and outstretched arm. Nothing is too hard for you. . . ." Then the word of the LORD came to Jeremiah: "I am the LORD, the God of all mankind. Is anything too hard for me?" (NIV)

### 3. See the glory and power of God.

1 Chronicles 29:10–13
1 Chronicles 29:11–12 Yours, O LORD, is the greatness and the power and the glory and the victory and the majesty, for all that is in the heavens and in the earth is yours. Yours is the kingdom, O LORD, and you are exalted as head above all. Both riches and honor come from you, and you rule over all. In your hand are power and might, and in your hand it is to make great and to give strength to all.

### 4. The Lord is your shepherd.

Psalm 23

5. **The Lord is the believer's light and his salvation.**

**Psalm 27** *(See the entire psalm; notice especially vv. 1, 2, 5, 7, 8, 13, 14.)*

**Psalm 27:8** You have said, "Seek my face." My heart says to you, "Your face, LORD, do I seek."

**Psalm 27:13–14** I believe that I shall look upon the goodness of the LORD in the land of the living! Wait for the LORD; be strong, and let your heart take courage; wait for the LORD!

6. **The Lord is the believer's refuge and strength.**

**Psalm 91:1–2** He who dwells in the shelter of the Most High will abide in the shadow of the Almighty. I will say to the LORD, "My refuge and my fortress, my God, in whom I trust!" (NASB)

7. **Lift your eyes to the hills.**

**Psalm 121** *(See the entire psalm, which teaches so beautifully that the Lord is our helper, the one who watches over us and keeps us.)*

8. **Jesus calmed the storm and rebuked the disciples for their little faith.**

**Matthew 8:23–27**

9. **Jesus rebuked Peter for his little faith.**

**Matthew 14:22–31** *(Jesus walked on water; Peter tried and failed.)*

**Matthew 14:31** Immediately Jesus reached out his hand and caught him. "You of little faith," he said, "why did you doubt?" (NIV)

10. **God is faithful; his mercies are new every morning.**

**Lamentations 3:22–24** Because of the LORD's great love we are not consumed, for his compassions never fail. They are new every morning; great is your faithfulness. I say to myself, "The LORD is my portion; therefore I will wait for him." (NIV)

11. **God is always faithful.**

Lamentations 3:32 Though he brings grief, he will show compassion, so great is his unfailing love. (NIV)

12. **Trust and delight in the Lord; wait patiently for him.**

Psalm 37:1–7
Psalm 37:3 Trust in the LORD and do good; dwell in the land and cultivate faithfulness. (NASB)
Psalm 37:4 Delight yourself in the LORD; and He will give you the desires of your heart. (NASB)
Psalm 37:5–6 Commit your way to the LORD, trust also in Him, and He will do it. He will bring forth your righteousness as the light and your judgment as the noonday. (NASB)
Psalm 37:7 Rest in the LORD and wait patiently for Him. (NASB)

13. **Why are you downcast? Hope in God!**

Psalm 42
Psalm 42:5 Why are you in despair, O my soul? And why have you become disturbed within me? Hope in God, for I shall again praise Him for the help of His presence. (NASB)

14. **God is our refuge and strength.**

Psalm 46

15. **God knows us intimately; he is always leading us.**

Psalm 139:1–11
Psalm 139:1–3 O LORD, you have searched me and known me! You know when I sit down and when I rise up; you discern my thoughts from afar. You search out my path and my lying down and are acquainted with all my ways.
Psalm 139:9–10 If I take the wings of the morning and dwell in the uttermost parts of the sea, even there your hand shall lead me, and your right hand shall hold me.

16. **God holds and guides us.**

**Psalm 73:23–24** Yet I still belong to you; you hold my right hand. You guide me with your counsel, leading me to a glorious destiny. (NLT)

17. **Be near to God, your refuge.**

**Psalm 73:28** But as for me, how good it is to be near God! I have made the Sovereign LORD my shelter, and I will tell everyone about the wonderful things you do. (NLT)

18. **God gives comfort to his people, and encourages them to put their trust in him.**

Isaiah 40

**Isaiah 40:11** Like a shepherd He will tend His flock, in His arms He will gather the lambs and carry them in His bosom; He will gently lead the nursing ewes. (NASB)

**Isaiah 40:28–31** Do you not know? Have you not heard? The Everlasting God, the LORD, the Creator of the ends of the earth does not become weary or tired. His understanding is inscrutable. He gives strength to the weary, and to him who lacks might He increases power. Though youths grow weary and tired, and vigorous young men stumble badly, yet those who wait for the LORD will gain new strength; they will mount up with wings like eagles, they will run and not get tired, they will walk and not become weary. (NASB)

19. **Do not fear; you are the Lord's child.**

**Isaiah 43:1–3** But now, O Jacob, listen to the LORD who created you. O Israel, the one who formed you says, "Do not be afraid, for I have ransomed you. I have called you by name; you are mine. When you go through deep waters, I will be with you. When you go through rivers of difficulty, you will not drown. When you walk through the fire of oppression, you will not be burned up; the flames will not consume you. For I am the LORD, your God, the Holy One of Israel, your Savior." (NLT)

20. **Do not fear; the Lord is with you.**

> Isaiah 41:10 Don't be afraid, for I am with you. Don't be discouraged, for I am your God. I will strengthen you and help you. I will hold you up with my victorious right hand. (NLT)

21. **Call upon the Lord in the day of trouble.**

> Psalm 50:15 Then call on me when you are in trouble, and I will rescue you, and you will give me glory. (NLT)

22. **Take refuge in the Lord.**

> Psalm 57:1 Be merciful to me, O God, be merciful to me, for in you my soul takes refuge; in the shadow of your wings I will take refuge, till the storms of destruction pass by.

23. **Trust your heavenly Father to take care of you. Think of how God cares even for the birds and the flowers. You are of much more value than they.**

> Matthew 6:25–34

24. **God's servant Joshua is given a difficult task. The Lord counsels him to be strong and courageous.**

> Joshua 1:1–9
> Joshua 1:9 Have I not commanded you? Be strong and courageous. Do not be afraid; do not be discouraged, for the LORD your God will be with you wherever you go. (NIV)

25. **Trust in the Lord brings peace to the heart. Trust in his unfailing love.**

> Isaiah 26:3–4 You will keep in perfect peace those whose minds are steadfast, because they trust in you. Trust in the LORD forever, for the LORD, the LORD himself, is the Rock eternal. (NIV)
> Psalm 9:9 The LORD is a refuge for the oppressed, a stronghold in times of trouble. (NIV)
> Psalm 28:7–8 The LORD is my strength and my shield; my heart trusts in him, and he helps me. My heart leaps for joy,

and with my song I praise him. The LORD is the strength of his people, a fortress of salvation for his anointed one. (NIV)

Psalm 33:18–22 Behold, the eye of the LORD is on those who fear him, on those who hope in his steadfast love, that he may deliver their soul from death and keep them alive in famine. Our soul waits for the LORD; he is our help and our shield. For our heart is glad in him, because we trust in his holy name. Let your steadfast love, O LORD, be upon us, even as we hope in you.

Psalm 36:5–9 Your steadfast love, O LORD, extends to the heavens, your faithfulness to the clouds. Your righteousness is like the mountains of God; your judgments are like the great deep; man and beast you save, O LORD. How precious is your steadfast love, O God! The children of mankind take refuge in the shadow of your wings. They feast on the abundance of your house, and you give them drink from the river of your delights. For with you is the fountain of life; in your light do we see light.

### 26. God cares for those who trust in him.

Nahum 1:7 The LORD is good, a refuge in times of trouble. He cares for those who trust in him. (NIV)

### 27. Do not trust in worldly power or wicked men.

Isaiah 31:1 Woe to those who go down to Egypt for help, who rely on horses, who trust in the multitude of their chariots and in the great strength of their horsemen, but do not look to the Holy One of Israel, or seek help from the LORD. (NIV)

Jeremiah 17:7–8 But blessed is the one who trusts in the LORD, whose confidence is in him. They will be like a tree planted by the water that sends out its roots by the stream. (NIV)

### 28. God cannot forget us.

Isaiah 49:14–16 But Zion said, "The LORD has forsaken me; my Lord has forgotten me." Can a woman forget her nursing child, that she should have no compassion on the son of her womb? Even these may forget, yet I will not forget you. Behold, I have engraved you on the palms of my hands; your walls are continually before me.

29. Find rest in God alone. Trust in him at all times, under any and all circumstances.

Psalm 62:5–8 My soul, wait silently for God alone, for my expectation is from Him. He only is my rock and my salvation; He is my defense; I shall not be moved. In God is my salvation and my glory; the rock of my strength, and my refuge, is in God. Trust in Him at all times, you people; pour out your heart before Him; God is a refuge for us. (NKJV)

30. The Lord takes delight in those who fear him and trust in his unfailing love.

Psalm 147:11 The LORD favors those who fear Him, those who wait for His lovingkindness. (NASB)

31. Keep trusting in God's unfailing love even when a desired blessing seems to be so slow, so long in coming.

Psalm 13
Psalm 13:1 How long, O LORD? Will You forget me forever? How long will You hide Your face from me? (NASB)
Psalm 13:5–6 But I have trusted in Your lovingkindness; my heart shall rejoice in Your salvation. I will sing to the LORD, because He has dealt bountifully with me. (NASB)

32. God's people were rebuked and judged for not trusting the Lord to bring them safely into the promised land after he had led them so marvelously on their pilgrim journey.

Deuteronomy 1:26–36
Deuteronomy 1:32–33 Yet in spite of this word you did not believe the LORD your God, who went before you in the way to seek you out a place to pitch your tents, in fire by night and in the cloud by day, to show you by what way you should go.

# Warnings, Calls to Repentance and Obedience

*See also* **Repentance, Obedience**

Note: Many warnings are coupled with promises from God to those who trust in him and serve him faithfully.

### 1. The way of sin leads to death; the way of obedience to life.

**Matthew 7:13–14** Enter through the narrow gate; for the gate is wide and the way is broad that leads to destruction, and there are many who enter through it. For the gate is small and the way is narrow that leads to life, and there are few who find it. (NASB)

### 2. Only those who hear and obey God's Word will have life.

**Matthew 7:21–23** Not everyone who says to Me, "Lord, Lord," will enter the kingdom of heaven, but he who does the will of My Father who is in heaven will enter. Many will say to Me on that day, "Lord, Lord, did we not prophesy in Your name, and in Your name cast out demons, and in Your name perform many miracles?" And then I will declare to them, "I never knew you; depart from Me, you who practice lawlessness." (NASB)

### 3. Jesus gave us the parable of the wise and the foolish builders.

**Matthew 7:24–27** Therefore everyone who hears these words of Mine and acts on them, may be compared to a wise man who built his house on the rock. And the rain fell, and the floods came, and the winds blew and slammed against that house; and yet it did not fall, for it had been founded on the rock. Everyone who hears these words of Mine and does not act on them, will be like a foolish man who built his house on the sand. The rain fell, and the floods came, and the winds blew and slammed against that house; and it fell—and great was its fall. (NASB)

### 4. You will reap what you sow.

**Proverbs 22:5** Corrupt people walk a thorny, treacherous road; whoever values life will avoid it. (NLT)

**Proverbs 11:19–21** Godly people find life; evil people find death. The LORD detests people with crooked hearts, but he delights in those with integrity. Evil people will surely be punished, but the children of the godly will go free. (NLT)

**Galatians 6:7–8** Do not be deceived, God is not mocked; for whatever a man sows, this he will also reap. For the one who sows to his own flesh will from the flesh reap corruption, but the one who sows to the Spirit will from the Spirit reap eternal life. (NASB)

### 5. No one can serve two masters—God will not accept a double life.

**Matthew 6:24** No one can serve two masters. Either you will hate the one and love the other, or you will be devoted to the one and despise the other. You cannot serve both God and money. (NIV)

### 6. God rejects the worship of one who is living in sin.

**Proverbs 15:8** The sacrifice of the wicked is an abomination to the LORD, but the prayer of the upright is His delight. (NASB)

**Proverbs 15:29** The LORD is far from the wicked, but He hears the prayer of the righteous. (NASB)

**Proverbs 21:27** The sacrifice of the wicked is an abomination, how much more when he brings it with evil intent! (NASB)

**Proverbs 28:9** He who turns away his ear from listening to the law, even his prayer is an abomination. (NASB)

### 7. If you keep ignoring God's call to repentance, he will laugh at your calamity.

**Proverbs 1:24–33**

8. **The Lord curses the wicked, but he blesses the righteous.**

Proverbs 3:33 The curse of the LORD is on the house of the wicked, but He blesses the dwelling of the righteous. (NASB)

9. **The wages of sin is death.**

Romans 6:23 The wages of sin is death, but the gift of God is eternal life in Christ Jesus our Lord. (NIV)

10. **We are warned not to drift away from the Lord.**

Hebrews 2:1–3 We must pay the most careful attention, therefore, to what we have heard, so that we do not drift away. For since the message spoken through angels was binding, and every violation and disobedience received its just punishment, how shall we escape if we ignore so great a salvation? This salvation, which was first announced by the Lord, was confirmed to us by those who heard him. (NIV)

11. **We are warned not to fall away.**

Hebrews 6:4–6 For it is impossible to bring back to repentance those who were once enlightened—those who have experienced the good things of heaven and shared in the Holy Spirit, who have tasted the goodness of the word of God and the power of the age to come—and who then turn away from God. It is impossible to bring such people back to repentance; by rejecting the Son of God, they themselves are nailing him to the cross once again and holding him up to public shame. (NLT)

12. **Those who have known the way but go on sinning are warned of the consequences.**

Hebrews 10:26–31
Hebrews 10:26–27 For if we go on sinning deliberately after receiving the knowledge of the truth, there no longer remains a sacrifice for sins, but a fearful expectation of judgment, and a fury of fire that will consume the adversaries.

Hebrews 10:31 It is a fearful thing to fall into the hands of the living God.

13. **Don't harden your heart; listen to his voice today.**

   **Hebrews 3:7–15**

   **Hebrews 3:7–8** As the Holy Spirit says: "Today, if you hear his voice, do not harden your hearts as you did in the rebellion." (NIV)

14. **On the judgment day Jesus will separate the sheep from the goats.**

   **Matthew 25:31–46**

   **Matthew 25:34** Then the King will say to those on his right, "Come, you who are blessed by my Father; take your inheritance, the kingdom prepared for you since the creation of the world." (NIV)

   **Matthew 25:41** Then he will say to those on his left, "Depart from me, you who are cursed, into the eternal fire prepared for the devil and his angels." (NIV)

   **Matthew 25:46** Then they will go away to eternal punishment, but the righteous to eternal life. (NIV)

15. **What if you gain the whole world and lose your soul?**

   **Matthew 16:26–27** For what will it profit a man if he gains the whole world and forfeits his life? Or what shall a man give in return for his life? For the Son of Man is going to come with his angels in the glory of his Father, and then he will repay each person according to what he has done.

16. **We will all appear before the judgment seat of Christ.**

   **2 Corinthians 5:10** For we must all appear before the judgment seat of Christ, that each one may receive the things done in the body, according to what he has done, whether good or bad. (NKJV)

17. **Always be prepared for Jesus' return, for the day and hour are not known.**

   **Mark 13:32–37** But of that day or hour no one knows, not even the angels in heaven, nor the Son, but the Father alone. Take heed, keep on the alert; for you do not know when the appointed time will come. It is like a man away on a journey, who upon leaving his house and putting his slaves in charge, assigning to each one his task, also commanded the doorkeeper to stay on the alert. Therefore, be on the alert—for you do not know when the master of the house is coming, whether in the evening, at midnight, or when the rooster crows, or in the morning—in case he should come suddenly and find you asleep. What I say to you I say to all, "Be on the alert!" (NASB)

18. Jesus gave us the parable of the ten virgins.

    Matthew 25:1–13

19. Only those who believe in Jesus will be saved.

    John 3:16–18 God so loved the world that he gave his one and only Son, that whoever believes in him shall not perish but have eternal life. For God did not send his Son into the world to condemn the world, but to save the world through him. Whoever believes in him is not condemned, but whoever does not believe stands condemned already because they have not believed in the name of God's one and only Son. (NIV)

20. Blessed is the man who does not walk in the way of the wicked. The wicked will not stand in the day of judgment.

    Psalm 1

21. God's judgment by the flood and the destruction of Sodom and Gomorrah are set forth as a warning to sinners today.

    2 Peter 2:4–10
    Jude 6–7, 14–15

22. The history of others is recorded as a warning for us.

    1 Corinthians 10:11–12 Now these things happened to them [Israelites] as an example, and they were written for our instruction, upon whom the ends of the ages have come. Therefore let him who thinks he stands take heed that he does not fall. (NASB)

23. **God punishes the guilty.**

**Nahum 1:1–6**
Nahum 1:2–3 The LORD is a jealous God, filled with vengeance and wrath. He takes revenge on all who oppose him and continues to rage against his enemies! The LORD is slow to get angry, but his power is great, and he never lets the guilty go unpunished. He displays his power in the whirlwind and the storm. The billowing clouds are the dust beneath his feet. (NLT)

24. **Woe to those who call evil good and good evil.**

Isaiah 5:20–21 What sorrow for those who say that evil is good and good is evil, that dark is light and light is dark, that bitter is sweet and sweet is bitter. What sorrow for those who are wise in their own eyes and think themselves so clever. (NLT)

25. **One who has known the Way but turns away from the Lord will receive greater condemnation.**

2 Peter 2:20–22 For if, after they have escaped the defilements of the world through the knowledge of our Lord and Savior Jesus Christ, they are again entangled in them and overcome, the last state has become worse for them than the first. For it would have been better for them never to have known the way of righteousness than after knowing it to turn back from the holy commandment delivered to them. What the true proverb says has happened to them: "The dog returns to its own vomit, and the sow, after washing herself, returns to wallow in the mire."

26. **Unrepented sin separates a person from God.**

Isaiah 59:1–2 Surely the arm of the LORD is not too short to save, nor his ear too dull to hear. But your iniquities have separated you from your God; your sins have hidden his face from you, so that he will not hear. (NIV)

27. **God detests hypocritical worship coupled with ungodly living.**

Jeremiah 7:1–29

**Jeremiah 7:2–4** Stand in the gate of the Lord's house, and proclaim there this word, and say, "Hear the word of the Lord, all you men of Judah who enter these gates to worship the Lord. Thus says the Lord of hosts, the God of Israel: Amend your ways and your deeds, and I will let you dwell in this place. Do not trust in these deceptive words: 'This is the temple of the Lord, the temple of the Lord, the temple of the Lord.'"

**Jeremiah 7:9–11** Will you steal, murder, commit adultery, swear falsely, make offerings to Baal, and go after other gods that you have not known, and then come and stand before me in this house, which is called by my name, and say, "We are delivered!"—only to go on doing all these abominations? Has this house, which is called by my name, become a den of robbers in your eyes? Behold, I myself have seen it, declares the Lord.

# Work, Laziness

1. **At the dawn of history God called man to work as his servant.**

   **Genesis 2:15** The LORD God took the man and put him in the Garden of Eden to work it and take care of it. (NIV)

2. **Be a workman approved of God.**

   **2 Timothy 2:15** Do your best to present yourself to God as one approved, a worker who does not need to be ashamed and who correctly handles the word of truth. (NIV)

3. **Do everything to the glory of God; perform your work in a way that glorifies him.**

   **1 Corinthians 10:31** Whether you eat or drink or whatever you do, do it all for the glory of God. (NIV)
   **Colossians 3:17** Whatever you do, whether in word or deed, do it all in the name of the Lord Jesus, giving thanks to God the Father through him. (NIV)

4. **An industrious housewife and mother pleases the Lord and delights her husband.**

   **Proverbs 31:10–31**

5. **Christians must work in order to give to others; never steal.**

   **Ephesians 4:28** Let the thief no longer steal, but rather let him labor, doing honest work with his own hands, so that he may have something to share with anyone in need.

6. Be a faithful worker so that you will be a good witness to outsiders and not be dependent on others.

1 Thessalonians 4:11–12 Make it your goal to live a quiet life, minding your own business and working with your hands, just as we instructed you before. Then people who are not Christians will respect the way you live, and you will not need to depend on others. (NLT)

7. Be on guard against idleness.

2 Thessalonians 3:6–15
2 Thessalonians 3:7–10 For you know that you ought to imitate us. We were not idle when we were with you. We never accepted food from anyone without paying for it. We worked hard day and night so we would not be a burden to any of you. We certainly had the right to ask you to feed us, but we wanted to give you an example to follow. Even while we were with you, we gave you this command: "Those unwilling to work will not get to eat." (NLT)

8. Earn your own bread.

2 Thessalonians 3:12 We command such people and urge them in the name of the Lord Jesus Christ to settle down and work to earn their own living. (NLT)

9. The ant provides a lesson for lazy, careless people.

Proverbs 6:6–11 Take a lesson from the ants, you lazybones. Learn from their ways and become wise! Though they have no prince or governor or ruler to make them work, they labor hard all summer, gathering food for the winter. But you, lazybones, how long will you sleep? When will you wake up? A little extra sleep, a little more slumber, a little folding of the hands to rest—then poverty will pounce on you like a bandit; scarcity will attack you like an armed robber. (NLT)

10. It's a disgrace to be lazy.

Proverbs 10:5 A wise youth harvests in the summer, but one who sleeps during harvest is a disgrace. (NLT)

11. One who chases fantasies lacks judgment.

Proverbs 12:11 A hard worker has plenty of food, but a person who chases fantasies has no sense. (NLT)

12. Mere talk leads to poverty.

Proverbs 14:23 Work brings profit, but mere talk leads to poverty! (NLT)

13. The way of the sluggard is hard.

Proverbs 15:19 The way of the lazy is as a hedge of thorns, but the path of the upright is a highway. (NASB)

14. The shiftless man goes hungry.

Proverbs 19:15 Laziness brings on deep sleep, and the shiftless go hungry. (NIV)

15. Being lazy has its sad results.

Proverbs 20:4 Sluggards do not plow in season; so at harvest time they look but find nothing. (NIV)

16. Do not love sleep.

Proverbs 20:13 Do not love sleep, or you will become poor; open your eyes, and you will be satisfied with food. (NASB)

17. A shiftless sluggard will come to poverty.

Proverbs 24:30–34 I walked by the field of a lazy person, the vineyard of one with no common sense. I saw that it was over-grown with nettles. It was covered with weeds, and its walls were broken down. Then, as I looked and thought about it, I learned this lesson: A little extra sleep, a little more slumber, a little folding of the hands to rest—then poverty will pounce on you like a bandit; scarcity will attack you like an armed robber. (NLT)

18. **The sluggard finds excuses not to work; he rationalizes his behavior.**

Proverbs 26:13–16 The lazy person claims, "There's a lion on the road! Yes, I'm sure there's a lion out there!" As a door swings back and forth on its hinges, so the lazy person turns over in bed. Lazy people take food in their hand but don't even lift it to their mouth. Lazy people consider themselves smarter than seven wise counselors. (NLT)

19. **The sleep of a laborer is sweet.**

Ecclesiastes 5:12 The sleep of a laborer is sweet, whether they eat little or much, but as for the rich, their abundance permits them no sleep. (NIV)

20. **In the parable of the talents Jesus teaches us to serve him faithfully with the talents he gives to us.**

Matthew 25:14–30

21. **One who fails to provide for his family denies the faith.**

1 Timothy 5:8 But if anyone does not provide for his relatives, and especially for members of his household, he has denied the faith and is worse than an unbeliever.

22. **We must learn to work so that we may provide for daily necessities and live productive lives.**

Titus 3:14 Our people must learn to do good by meeting the urgent needs of others; then they will not be unproductive. (NLT)

# Worry, Anxiety

*See also* Prayer, Trust

1. **Jesus instructs us not to worry about tomorrow; about food, clothing, etc.**

   **Matthew 6:25–34**
   **Matthew 6:25** Therefore I tell you, do not be anxious about your life, what you will eat or what you will drink, nor about your body, what you will put on. Is not life more than food, and the body more than clothing?
   **Matthew 6:26–28** Look at the birds of the air: they neither sow nor reap nor gather into barns, and yet your heavenly Father feeds them. Are you not of more value than they? And which of you by being anxious can add a single hour to his span of life? And why are you anxious about clothing? Consider the lilies of the field, how they grow: they neither toil nor spin.

2. **Take one day at a time, and don't borrow trouble.**

   **Matthew 6:34** Therefore do not be anxious about tomorrow, for tomorrow will be anxious for itself. Sufficient for the day is its own trouble.

3. **Don't be anxious, but pray.**

   **Philippians 4:6–7** Don't worry about anything; instead, pray about everything. Tell God what you need, and thank him for all he has done. Then you will experience God's peace, which exceeds anything we can understand. His peace will guard your hearts and minds as you live in Christ Jesus. (NLT)

4. Cast all your anxiety on the Lord.

1 Peter 5:6–7 Humble yourselves, therefore, under the mighty hand of God so that at the proper time he may exalt you, casting all your anxieties on him, because he cares for you.

5. You can discover the secret of tranquility.

Psalm 37:3–7
Psalm 37:3 Trust in the LORD and do good. (NIV)
Psalm 37:4 Take delight in the LORD. (NIV)
Psalm 37:5 Commit your way to the LORD. (NIV)
Psalm 37:7 Be still before the LORD and wait patiently for him. (NIV)

6. Anxiety weighs a person down.

Proverbs 12:25 Anxiety in a man's heart weighs it down, but a good word makes it glad. (NASB)

Proverbs 14:30 A tranquil heart is life to the body, but passion is rottenness to the bones. (NASB)

Proverbs 17:22 A joyful heart is good medicine, but a broken spirit dries up the bones. (NASB)

# Youth

*See also* Forgiveness of Sins, Friendships, Warnings

### 1. Be happy, young man.

Ecclesiastes 11:9–10 Rejoice, young man, during your childhood, and let your heart be pleasant during the days of young manhood. And follow the impulses of your heart and the desires of your eyes. Yet know that God will bring you to judgment for all these things. So, remove grief and anger from your heart and put away pain from your body, because childhood and the prime of life are fleeting. (NASB)

### 2. Remember your Creator in the days of your youth.

Ecclesiastes 12:1 Remember also your Creator in the days of your youth, before the evil days come and the years draw near when you will say, "I have no delight in them." (NASB)

### 3. Be sure to go God's way.

Proverbs 3:1–4 My child, never forget the things I have taught you. Store my commands in your heart. If you do this, you will live many years, and your life will be satisfying. Never let loyalty and kindness leave you! Tie them around your neck as a reminder. Write them deep within your heart. Then you will find favor with both God and people, and you will earn a good reputation. (NLT)

### 4. Trust in the Lord; acknowledge him in all your ways.

Proverbs 3:5–6 Trust in the LORD with all your heart; do not depend on your own understanding. Seek his will in all you do, and he will show you which path to take. (NLT)

5. **The fear of the Lord is the beginning of knowledge and wisdom.**

**Proverbs 1:7** The fear of the LORD is the beginning of knowledge, but fools despise wisdom and instruction. (NKJV)

**Proverbs 9:10–11** The fear of the LORD is the beginning of wisdom, and the knowledge of the Holy One is understanding. For by me your days will be multiplied, and years of life will be added to you. (NKJV)

**Proverbs 15:33** The fear of the LORD is the instruction of wisdom, and before honor is humility. (NKJV)

6. **Fools despise instruction.**

**Proverbs 1:7** The fear of the LORD is the beginning of knowledge, but fools despise wisdom and instruction. (NKJV)

**Proverbs 13:13** He who despises the word will be destroyed, but he who fears the commandment will be rewarded. (NKJV)

7. **Listen to parental instruction for your own good.**

**Proverbs 1:8–9** My son, hear the instruction of your father, and do not forsake the law of your mother; for they will be a graceful ornament on your head, and chains about your neck. (NKJV)

**Proverbs 4:1–4** Hear, O sons, a father's instruction, and be attentive, that you may gain insight, for I give you good precepts; do not forsake my teaching. When I was a son with my father, tender, the only one in the sight of my mother, he taught me and said to me, "Let your heart hold fast my words; keep my commandments, and live."

**Proverbs 6:20–24** My son, keep your father's command, and do not forsake the law of your mother. Bind them continually upon your heart; tie them around your neck. When you roam, they will lead you; when you sleep, they will keep you; and when you awake, they will speak with you. For the commandment is a lamp, and the law a light; reproofs of instruction are the way of life, to keep you from the evil woman, from the flattering tongue of a seductress. (NIV)

8. **Don't despise the Lord's discipline, for he disciplines those he loves (and parents must follow his example).**

   **Proverbs 3:11–12** My son, do not despise the Lord's discipline or be weary of his reproof, for the Lord reproves him whom he loves, as a father the son in whom he delights.
   **Hebrews 12:5–11**

9. **He who hates correction is stupid.**

   **Proverbs 12:1** Whoever loves discipline loves knowledge, but whoever hates correction is stupid. (NIV)

10. **Don't ignore discipline; be thankful for it.**

    **Proverbs 13:18** Poverty and disgrace come to him who ignores instruction, but whoever heeds reproof is honored.
    **Proverbs 15:5** A fool despises his father's instruction, but whoever heeds reproof is prudent.
    **Proverbs 15:12** A scoffer does not like to be reproved; he will not go to the wise.
    **Proverbs 15:31–32** The ear that listens to life-giving reproof will dwell among the wise. Whoever ignores instruction despises himself, but he who listens to reproof gains intelligence.

11. **Love requires discipline.**

    Whoever spares the rod hates their children, but the one who loves their children is careful to discipline them. (NIV)

12. **If others entice you, don't consent or yield.**

    **Proverbs 1:10–19**
    **Proverbs 1:10** My son, if sinful men entice you, do not give in to them. (NIV)
    **Proverbs 1:15** My son, do not go along with them, do not set foot on their paths. (NIV)

13. **Avoid the path of the wicked; turn far from it.**

    Proverbs 4:14–15 Do not enter the path of the wicked, and do not walk in the way of the evil. Avoid it; do not go on it; turn away from it and pass on.

14. **Stand firm; don't be willy-nilly; don't be moved.**

    1 Corinthians 15:58 Therefore, my beloved brethren, be steadfast, immovable, always abounding in the work of the Lord, knowing that your toil is not in vain in the Lord. (NASB)

15. **Be a valiant soldier of Jesus Christ; use God's armor.**

    Ephesians 6:10–18
    Ephesians 6:10–11 Finally, be strong in the Lord and in the strength of His might. Put on the full armor of God, so that you will be able to stand firm against the schemes of the devil. (NASB)

16. **Joseph, the young man, stands as a good example for us.**

    Genesis 39 *(Even when Joseph was far from home, a slave in Egypt, he was strong in faith and godliness. He was willing to suffer for the Lord, rather than to sin against him. When Potiphar's wife tempted him, he would not yield to her demands.)*
    Genesis 39:9–10 "No one is greater in this house than I am. My master has withheld nothing from me except you, because you are his wife. How then could I do such a wicked thing and sin against God?" And though she spoke to Joseph day after day, he refused to go to bed with her or even be with her. (NIV)

17. **Daniel also is a good example to follow. As a young man he was carried off to Babylon. There he remained faithful to God at all costs.**

    Daniel 1:8–9 But Daniel resolved not to defile himself with the royal food and wine, and he asked the chief official for permission not to defile himself this way. Now God had caused the official to show favor and compassion to Daniel. (NIV)

Daniel 6 *(Even when he knew that he would be thrown into the den of lions, Daniel kept on praying to his God, against the king's decree.)*

Daniel 6:10 Now when Daniel learned that the decree had been published, he went home to his upstairs room where the windows opened toward Jerusalem. Three times a day he got down on his knees and prayed, giving thanks to his God, just as he had done before. (NIV)

18. **The three friends of Daniel also remained faithful to God at all costs.**

Daniel 3
Daniel 3:16–18 Shadrach, Meshach and Abed-nego replied to the king, "O Nebuchadnezzar, we do not need to give you an answer concerning this matter. If it be so, our God whom we serve is able to deliver us from the furnace of blazing fire; and He will deliver us out of your hand, O king. But even if He does not, let it be known to you, O king, that we are not going to serve your gods or worship the golden image that you have set up." (NASB)

19. **Honor your father and mother.**

Exodus 20:12 Honor your father and your mother, that your days may be long upon the land which the LORD your God is giving you. (NKJV)

20. **Honor and obey your parents.**

Ephesians 6:1–3 Children, obey your parents in the Lord, for this is right. "Honor your father and mother"—which is the first commandment with a promise—"so that it may go well with you and that you may enjoy long life on the earth" [Deut. 5:16]. (NIV)

Colossians 3:20 Children, obey your parents in everything, for this pleases the Lord. (NIV)

21. **Jesus was obedient to his parents.**

Luke 2:51 And he went down with them and came to Nazareth and was submissive to them. And his mother treasured up all these things in her heart.

22. **Flee the evil desires of youth.**

2 Timothy 2:22 So flee youthful passions and pursue righteousness, faith, love, and peace, along with those who call on the Lord from a pure heart.